Things Church Girls Don't Talk About

SUSAN SIEWEKE

authorHOUSE®

AuthorHouse™
1663 Liberty Drive
Bloomington, IN 47403
www.authorhouse.com
Phone: 1-800-839-8640

Published by AuthorHouse 8/3/2012

ISBN: 978-1-4685-5533-2 (sc)
ISBN: 978-1-4685-5532-5 (hc)
ISBN: 978-1-4685-5531-8 (e)

Library of Congress Control Number: 2012903315

A Novel
For those who don't like organized religion and for those who do

Things Church Girls Don't Talk About

CHAPTER 1

A BUDDING CHURCH GIRL

I BECAME A CHURCH GIRL in nineteen-sixty-something when I walked the aisle in a little Southern Baptist church to the umpteenth verse of the hymn, "Just as I Am." It's a fine song with a catchy tune, but after the third time through—even Mother Theresa would get testy.

Walking the aisle is what you do when you want to *get* saved. "Saved from *what?*" you might be thinking. Saved from Hell. H-E-Double-L. I will never forget that day; how could I? The memory's etched in my brain like a poison pitchfork.

It happened on a serious Sunday morning in a little church called Grace and Truth. There we were—Mama and I in our Sunday best; the perfect back row Baptists. Our dainty legs crossed at the knee. Our patent leather shoes shining like new money. And even though the pastor had been speaking for well over an hour, still we were all ears as we listened attentively to his passionate preaching.

The man was excitable. High-strung as a mad dog caged at the pound. He paced up and down behind the podium so fast it was making my head swim. And then, in the midst of his frenzy, he pointed his shaming paw in our faces and told every last one of us that we'd better turn or burn.

Remembering my feelings that day, a predominant one stands out in my mind.

Fear.

Oh, Lord have mercy! This red-headed, freckled-faced child was scared out of my wits. And for a darn good reason. The minister was—can a church girl even say it?

Mean as Hell.

Cold chills crawled up and down my spine as he threatened us with gory stories about people who died and went to their eternal punishment because they refused to get saved. The preacher's descriptions of hellfire and damnation were vivid. Wailing and gnashing of teeth. Rolling waves of molten lava. Demons spewing fire from their nostrils like angry medieval dragons.

I tell you the truth, after hearing these tales of horror, my poor heart started beating like a humming bird's. Ninety miles an hour. I thought it was gonna jump out of my chest. I felt dizzy. Sick to my stomach. Sweat was popping out on my forehead. Meanwhile, the choir (oblivious to my panic attack), just kept on crooning that haunting tune. . . .

Just as I am without one plea, but that thy blood was shed for me,
and that thou bids me come to thee
O Lamb of God I come.....

"Blood? Lambs? Dear God," I thought to myself, "this is getting more tragic by the minute." And then, before I could gain composure, the religious terrorist started in on us again by quoting frightening excerpts from Jonathan Edward's sermon, "Sinners in the Hands of an Angry God."

He is not only able to cast wicked men into Hell, but he can
most easily, do it...The old serpent is gasping for them; Hell
opens its mouth wide to receive them; and, if God should
permit it, they would be hastily swallowed up and lost. . .

"Swallowed? Lost? Stop!" I screamed inside my mind. "I'll believe anything you want me to believe. You are right. I'm a sinner. A horrible, terrible, wicked sinner!"

And then, to be on the safe side, I started confessing my sins up to date. The time I changed the grade on my quiz from an "F" to a "B". The time I stole a hot ball from the corner grocery store. The time I played "show me yours, I'll show you mine" with the boys down the block. As the preacher worked the congregation, all of my wrongs passed before my eyes. I could not escape the conviction. There was nowhere to hide.

> *There is not a created thing not manifest before Him, but all things are naked and open to His eyes—with whom is our reckoning.*

Busted.

The minister was right. I was e-ville. Ready to split Hell wide open.

But as wicked as I was, as guilty as I felt at that moment, there was a part of me that secretly wondered if God was really as mean as that man made Him sound. Perhaps the preacher had exaggerated? Was there a remote possibility that God was just a wee bit nicer? But what if He wasn't? What if that preacher was right? What was this little church girl going to do with a mean God like *that* after salvation?

While everything in me was wishing that he would stop, the madman continued.

> *If you died in your sleep tonight, do you know for sure that you would not wake up in that fiery place reserved for the devil and his fallen angels? While the choir sings, just slip out of the pew, walk the aisle and escape the pit of darkness, the judgment by fire!*

And this he shouted while strapping on his Martin guitar so that he could strum along with the choir. Figuring I'd better be safe than sorry, I decided to give him what he wanted and get my Hell insurance. Yep. I was gonna do it. I was going to mind that preacher and escape eternal damnation at the same time. And so, with all the courage I had left in my frail, trembling body, I opened my eyes, took a deep breath, bolted out of the pew, ran down the aisle, and *got saved.*

And there you have it—my sad salvation story.

On that fearful day, I was saved from Hell and became a church girl. From the mentorship of my mama, I learned the churchy protocol—how to stand, how to sit, and how to cry without even smudging my make-up. I also learned how to tell little white lies to cover how I was *really* feeling if anyone should ask me how I was doing in church.

Additionally, I learned the friendly phrase the congregation used to give the impression of super-duper spirituality—"I'm blessed and highly favored." Have you heard it?

"How are you, Sister Sue?"

"Blessed and highly favored."

"But I heard that your son Jim Bob's in jail and your Mama's in a diabetic coma."

"Doesn't matter. I'm blessed and highly favored."

"How about you, Maybelle? Are you cryin' because your granny died?"

"Nope. I'm too spiritual to cry, you idiot. I'm too blessed and highly frickin' favored!"

But even in this *blessed and highly favored* state, I had a million unanswered questions: questions about God, the Bible, anything that pertained to spirituality. I had always been an inquiring girl when it came to matters of the heart, and I took that curious mind and personality into that little Baptist church in Birmingham, Alabama.

There was only one problem. The church didn't *like* my curious mind. They didn't *want* to know what was swirling around in my head. They were not the least bit interested in my questions. Particularly the one I asked one memorable Sunday about Thelma Lou Cratchett.

Thelma was a tall, lanky woman, country as a turnip, with short black hair and an intensely guilty look about her. She sat at the back of the church in the last pew and every Sunday she rededicated her life to God. I lie not. Every sanctified Sunday. I was no math whiz, but I figured it took Thelma only three days after her rededication before she was sinning again and again and again.

At the tender age of nine, I wondered what in the world the poor woman was doing that made her feel bad enough to run down the aisle and collapse weeping on the shoulder of the preacher every blessed Sunday. In my childish mind, I imagined all sorts of terrible things—cheating on her husband, stealing quarters from the offering plate; God only knows what this woman was doing!

As I sat quietly in the pew alongside my dear mama, I could count the verses of a hymn and predict when Thelma would be rededicating. After about six months of this same ol', same ol', when I was about to die from curiosity, I finally got up the nerve to ask about Thelma Lou in children's

Sunday school class. The lesson that day was about repentance. Miss Linda, the pious preacher's wife, opened up the class with a question.

"Does anyone know what repentance is?"

I stuck my hand up in the air and waved it wildly. "I do, Miss Linda, I do! I do!"

"Yes, Maggie, what is it?"

"It's what Thelma Lou does when she runs down the aisle every Sunday. It's her way of saying she's sorry for her sins," I said, confident that I had gotten the correct answer.

But then, instead of being content to just to see the approving look on Miss Linda's face, I had to push the envelope; take it to the limit. Instead of controlling myself, I'll be darned if my unruly tongue didn't set on fire the course of Hell by asking one of my nosey questions.

"But what are her sins, Miss Linda? Do you think that she has a cheating heart? Mama and I were thinking that she might be fooling around on her husband like those wicked women on the soap operas by doing it with Bubba in the choir room. Could that be her sin?"

As you can imagine, Miss Linda, the quintessential church girl, went off on me in front of God and everybody with that shrill, brutal voice of hers saying how unbecoming it was for me to be talking like that in front of Christian children.

"Well, I never! Didn't your mama raise you better than that?" Miss Linda huffed.

Then, standing herself up saintly straight while cocking her skinny hand on her waist like a teapot, she continued her tirade.

"How unbecoming! How *very unbecoming* it is for you to be talking like this in front of Christian children, you rude and brazen little girl! There's no excuse for you. No excuse at all. You need to mind your manners!"

And after her arrogant tell off, she had the nerve to point her boney finger in my face and howl at the top of her lungs, "I'm telling you for the *very* last time...

these are things church girls just don't talk about!"

CHAPTER 2

KISS MY BUTT AND CALL ME RUDY

AFTER THE PREACHER'S WIFE TOLD me it was inappropriate to be asking about Thelma Lou, I went home after church and told Mama what happened in Sunday school. When she heard my story she was madder than a wet hen. "If that preacher's wife thinks that she is going to tell my daughter what she can and can't say," Mama said, "she's barking up the wrong tree. The next time I see her I have half a mind to tell her to *kiss my butt and call me Rudy.*"

"Kiss my butt and call me Rudy." This was Mama's favorite saying when she was letting someone know that she was offended. As a youngster, I tried to make sense of it but I couldn't. Who *in the heck* is Rudy? Thankfully, Mama withheld that crude remark because to say that to a preacher's wife would have made my situation at the church even worse. I found out at an early age that when religious people get offended they could be as cruel and as callous as any unbelieving person alive.

God forgive me for saying this but Miss Linda was sorely lacking in humility. She walked around with her nose stuck up in the air like she was some holier-than-thou gospel goddess. As Jesus put it, "she gagged at gnats and swallowed camels," which means (if you're from southern Israel) that her religion was about as useful as goose shit on a pump handle. She put too much importance on things that didn't matter to a hill of beans. And sadly, in all the years I spent in her Sunday school class, this self-righteous matron never changed. She remained the same unloving, uptight person she was from the very first day I met her.

Unlike Miss Linda who weighed every word that came out of her mouth, Mama was raw in her unrestrained, colorful, way of expression. Feisty and darn proud of it, she taught me something most Southern women are *not* taught to do—speak their mind.

A no-no in the South.

If you are not familiar with this aspect of Southern culture, let me fill you in. Communication among women in the South is almost always done with a forced smile in the tradition of Southern Hospitality. And the two cardinal rules of Southern Hospitality are these: B: Bestow upon the recipient of your communication flattery due a queen. S: Side step the truth by *never* saying what you are really thinking and feeling so that you will *never* hurt anyone's feelings.

In other words—B.S. if you have to.

So, in retrospect when I asked Miss Linda about Thelma Lou, I know now I should have been a white liar and said the following: "Miss Linda, honey, darlin', sugar, sweetie, since you are the prettiest Sunday school teacher *evaaah*, I was wondering if it would not hurt your precious little feelings as to tell me why Miss Thelma Lou rededicates her life every Sunday? And if perhaps, she ain't fooling around with Bubba in the choir room? I need details so I can put her on my prayer list."

Do you see how this follows the two rules? As an aside, almost any attempt to rummage through someone's dirty laundry will be graciously granted if it is disguised as a prayer request!

Just my luck, this insight about Southern Hospitality came years too late, so I've had to live with the unanswered question about Thelma Lou and with the realization that I was far too forthright for those religious folk. But, to be fair to myself, I'll tell you now, it was not entirely my fault. Most of the blame belongs where most daughters love to put the blame. And where would that be?

On their mothers, of course.

So, let me tell you a little more about mine, the interesting woman who did not want to be called by the first name in her charming Southern double-name, Mary Careen, because she was named after her older sister,

Mary Justine and her mother, Mary Rose and hearing *those* names stirred up a hornet's nest of unresolved issues.

Mama was...and I say this with all of the sass that is in me . . . an *aspiring* Southern belle.

Pleased to be born and bred below the Mason-Dixon Line, Mama often bragged on herself, her upbringing, and her cooking as if she were the only woman in the world who could fry chicken, cream potatoes, and shell butterbeans without the help of a maid. A bit quirky in personality, she owned a life-size portrait of Scarlett O'Hara that she proudly displayed in our dining room along with an autographed copy of *Gone with the Wind*. Her mother, Mary Rose, whom I called Nana, was responsible for that *treasure* having been presented it to Mama on the day of her birth in 1940, long before she could read and find out that her middle name was the same as one of Scarlett's sisters. Much like that raven-haired beauty, Mama was dramatic, histrionic and the natural center of attention whenever she could make an audience out of friends or strangers.

In addition to her magnetism, Mama was a mighty fine example of a church girl. Thanks to her Baptist upbringing, she could recite all the books of the Bible by heart and quote scripture with the best of them. She had a drawer full of Sunday school pins and a closet full of hats which she sported on the first Sunday of the month—a ritual she stuck to even when it was no longer fashionable.

While we are on the subject, I need to mention that (just like Scarlett) Mama was good at keeping up appearances. Passionate about image and etiquette, she always minded her manners by never blowing her nose into a napkin, never tilting back her chair at the supper table, and always remembering to send "thank you" notes for any kindness, large or small. Furthermore, as a good Southern woman, Mama had her hair done once a week at the beauty shop whether it needed it or not, in the style of the iconic movie stars of the 1940's—Rita Hayworth, Bette Davis or Vivien Leigh, of course. One more thing. She *never ever* went shopping without lipstick on, ever mindful that opportunities to climb the social ladder might be just around the corner.

And if these incredible Southernisms weren't enough, my mesmerizing mama played the *piano*.

Even with all of her wonderfully winsome qualities, Mama still had her weaknesses. All of her good points could not obscure the fact that Mama was an incessant talker with the gift for gab that got on most folks last nerve—including mine. Some crude Southerners would say that she had diarrhea of the mouth.

Yes, even Mama would admit that her mouth could be her ruin.

Mama was an avid talker and painfully honest; blunt to the point of being offensive. And this, dear people, made her an oddity among church girls and destroyed her chances of ever being a *true* Southern Belle. Instead of being a sweet little apple dumpling with her conversation, Careen was a no nonsense, butter beans and cornbread woman who liked to tell it like it was. Call a spade—a spade. Mama wouldn't dare do the usual Southern thing like telling little white lies for social propriety's sake. Oh, no. She dared to tell the truth at any occasion and at any setting.

For instance, when the preacher's wife walked up to her in church one Sunday and asked… "Careen, how do you like my new hat?"

Mama, (seeing that her new hat made her look like a wind-blown cockatiel) replied… "It would be great to wear at the Audubon Society, but it's not *you*, Linda. You'd look much better without one!"

"Well, well, Careen," Linda said with her snooty little mouth… "Then how do you like the color of my new pink designer dress?"

To which Mama replied, "To be quite honest, Linda dear, it reminds me of a bottle of Pepto-Bismol, but if you like it that's all that matters."

As you can plainly see, Mama did not behave in the real Southern way.

Similarly, when Mama and I first attended a Wednesday night supper at Grace and Truth Baptist, one of the well-established women of the congregation, Savannah Culpepper, came up to her and said…

"Now, Careen, dear, it has been a blessing meeting you and your charming little girl. I'd love for all of us to get together. Y'all come to see me, anytime, ya hear."

Then, Mama (not realizing that the woman was phony boloney) took the statement at face value and said, "I'll go get my calendar so we can plan a time to get together."

But, when that woman saw that Mama was serious about getting together, a look crawled across her face like she'd been sucking on raw lemons. You would have thought that Mama had asked to borrow

Savannah's checkbook. The woman started backing away from Mama as if she were leprous.

It was in that moment that I saw the truth. Savannah had no intention of developing a friendship with us. She was full of it! The "S" word—*superficiality*. She did not mean a word she said. She was simply mouthing pleasantries to give the appearance of warmth and caring. And why? Glad you asked.

Because in the South—image is everything.

But Mama being the kind of gutsy gal she was, wouldn't stand for that. That angry woman stormed across the sanctuary in those spiked pointy-toed heels, tapped Savannah roughly on the shoulder and said…

"Now wait a minute *Missy*, hasn't anyone ever taken you up on your insincere offer before? I'm coming over to your house for supper whether you like it or not! And after dessert, we'll sit down together and read what it says about hypocrites in the Bible!"

In this one interchange, my mother broke every unspoken Southern rule in the book. So the next week, after Mama's encounter with Savannah— Savannah's daughter, Lonnie Sue, walked up to me in church and asked:

"Maggie, how do you like my new hair bow?"

And me, seeing that her new hair bow made her look like a show poodle, replied, "I wouldn't even wear it to a dog show. Wouldn't pay fifteen cents for it, girl!"

Lonnie Sue frowned and tried again. "But, Maggie, you just *have to* like my new brown dress."

"No, I don't just *have to* like it; the color looks like the inside of a diaper," I replied, "but if you like it, that's all that matters…dearie."

Like mother, like daughter.

And if having a tactless Mama wasn't enough to irritate the stew out of church people, another thing that made me a misfit in Southern church culture was the way I spoke. When I was seven my father moved our family to his hometown of Boston for the year so that he could study Bostonian History during his sabbatical. Unfortunately, being around all of those Yankee children rubbed off on me and diluted my Southern accent.

When we moved back to Alabama, little did I know that because of my northern enunciations, I would be persecuted. This is why I always say,

"Young'uns who are *born* in the South should *stay* in the South." My father did me a terrible disservice. Without the drawl, you're no one at all.

Seeing that I was having trouble getting along with my peers, Miss Linda confided in me in Sunday school class that the church girls considered my northern-ish accent hoity-toity. She said they thought that by talking this way I was acting like Miss Priss who was shore above her raisin'.

Well, being a people pleaser and desperately wanting to fit in, I immediately went to work to reverse the damage done by the Yankees. Determined that my Southern accent would rise again, I littered my conversations with *y'all's* and made two syllable words out of one syllable words. Quit became "quee-it." Next, I went to work on "I" sounds. "I" became "eye" or something like that. Each day, I practiced the new phonetics with commitment. I rehearsed the phrase, "Nice white ice" until I had it down: "Nice white ice. . . nice white ice. . . nice white ice."

Then I became ambitious and put together a whole sentence that I could say it in Sunday school. So, when Chester Nichols had finished his crackers and co-cola during snack time and started chomping on the ice in the bottom of his cup, I showed out with my newfound Southern accent.

"Quee-it chompin' on that niiihce whiiite iiice, Chestaa. You're makin' me e-yull!"

When she heard my dreadful drawl, Miss Linda looked at me as if I were Satan's sister. Then, the sinister saint sent me out of the room because she thought I was making fun of *her* accent. "You better quit mocking your elders, you rude and brazen little girl!" she said, sourly.

Rejected again!

Even with the return of my twang, I still found no acceptance among the girls in Sunday school even though I was as Southern as pear preserves on a homemade biscuit. Then, to make matters worse, the following week, I made the grave mistake of asking Miss Linda about Thelma Lou again. And as you may have guessed, this sealed my fate as an outcast at Grace and Truth Baptist Church. There was no grace for this church girl at that fellowship and that was the truth.

And so, in honor of the girls in Sunday school, in honor of those persnickety folks from the Deep South in the Bible belt who dared to ridicule my accent...as Mama used to say:

"Kiss my butt and call me Rudy!"

CHAPTER 3

ORPHANS AND MARRIED WIDOWS

My full name is Mary Margaret McBride and I was born and raised in the heart of Dixie in the great state of Alabama.

Pleased to meet you.

When you say it right it just rolls off your tongue as sweet as sorghum syrup. Alabama. Can you hear the Southern in it? Say it with me—A-la-bammmma. If you can't say it just like that, it "just ain't right," as they say in my stompin' ground. Unfortunately, poor grammar abounds in "Bama" even if you are from the charming city of Homewood, a suburb of Birmingham where Vulcan raises his fiery torch.

To tell the truth, I always thought that the huge cast iron statue was horribly demonic, the same sentiment that Mama had about our then Governor, George Wallace, before he was born again. Unlike some mistaken Alabamians who thought that the man hung the moon, Mama was quick to let it be known that the man was a racist and that she much preferred John F. Kennedy, whom she hero-worshipped. Politics were very important to Mama, and she tried to stay up on the subject when she wasn't catering after my father.

I remember the day that President Kennedy was assassinated even though I was just a child. On that terrible day, Mama stood in the living room watching reruns of the assassination until suppertime—wringing her hands and crying like her heart would break. Until this day, scenes from the news clips of that day float across my mind in black and white and I can still feel the hopelessness that Mama expressed. "Where were you when you heard about Kennedy's assassination?" was the question that the teachers in our school system asked the children for years to come. My answer to that question was that I was tucked safely away in my two-story birth home, nestled in the southern flank of the Red Mountain. It was a lovely house in Spanish Colonial Revival style, decorated with mostly Mediterranean furniture, antiques and a few contemporary pieces thrown in the mix. Mama loved color, so every room was vibrant, just like her personality. It was the perfect home for a professors wife and she was always entertaining folks from the college. On any given Saturday morning, I could walk into our living room and see her sitting with the group of professors' wives sipping tea, eating homemade blueberry muffins, and telling stories. Stories about Jim Crow. Stories about Martin Luther King. Stories about the Civil Rights protests. And, of course, stories about her favorite *handsome* President, John Fitzgerald Kennedy.

Homewood was just a hop, skip and a jump from The University of Alabama at Birmingham where my father taught history. Our town was also just a hop, skip and a jump from that Southern Baptist church and that darn preacher who was determined to save me from going to Hell.

Thinking back to when I first became a church girl, it's no wonder that God and I got off to a bad start. Just when I was about to recover from the trauma of the "Sinners in the Hands of an Angry God" sermon, here came the rules and demands of organized religion.

Jesus said that His yoke was easy and His burden was light. But, as far as I could tell, the church didn't believe that. They piled on the yokes as if they'd never read His words. Yokes of legalism. Yokes of performance. Rules by the numbers. Read your Bible every day. Don't forget to Pray. Don't drink. Don't cuss. Don't chew. And don't hang out with those who do. Woe be to the person who couldn't live up to the church's expectations. You were accused of either being weak or having sin in your life. Or both.

So, in an effort avoid the spiritual scrutiny, Mama and I tried to look as happy as possible whenever we went to church which was difficult since we had to listen to Pastor Smith tell us how wicked we were every week. But behind our Sunday faces, things weren't all that great regardless of how proper we appeared. Beneath our blessed and highly favored façade, we were sad, tormented little women because after church we had to go home and live with my phantom father, Martin McBride.

Dr. Martin McBride was a remote, orderly, college professor with a Ph.D. He possessed all the intellectual snobbery of Darwin and C.S. Lewis combined. A professed agnostic, he prided himself on the fact that he was not sure that God existed which made him appear more classy and open-minded than the awful atheists who were certain He did not.

Bottom line—he was a *heathen*.

Martin's passions were world history and red wine. As if teaching the subject five times a week at the college wasn't enough, when he came home from work the first thing he did was grab a bottle of burgundy and seclude himself in his office where he read "Mein Kampf" for probably the hundredth time. Comfortable and buzzed, he lost himself in the political ideology of Adolph Hitler—an obsession that got on Mama's last nerve.

Yes, Martin fled into the false refuge of his books as completely as he fled into the false refuge of the bottle. It seemed to me that he loved reading and drinking because it took him away from the here and now—from his duty as a husband and father. I don't think I can recall the look of my father's face in a full front view. All I see in my mind's eye is his profile; head bowed, gazing intently through his outdated wire-rimmed glasses into the pages of a hardback. Martin's emotional unavailability made Mama and me what we were—a married widow and an orphan.

Oh, the devilish wounds of married widows and orphans! Old wounds that bled in the hearts of generations of women before us who lived with this generational curse. Wounds that oozed like angry sap down our family tree staining everything it touched—their hopes and dreams, their doubts and faith, their happiness and their sorrow. Old, festering, bitter wounds that were painstakingly inflicted by the men folk in their lives who reminded their women every day of their lives that they were inferior. Wounds from bad, insecure, controlling men who were probably secretly irritated that women had won the right to vote.

The wounds of a married widow are awful indeed.

As the devils would have it, this unholy blood trickled down through the generations, transfusing its sick curse into our spirit, soul and body. Every day of my childhood, I lived this curse. I watched father arrive home from work with briefcase in hand, walk lifelessly through the kitchen door, mutter his perfunctory "Hello" and retreat to his office where he drank, watched TV and read until suppertime. Any conversation Mama tried to initiate before he secluded himself was met by angry discounting tones designed to let her know that she was an interruption to his thought life, to his reading, to his drinking and his date with Walter Cronkite on the evening news.

After numerous attempts to break into my father's carefully guarded world, Mama would resign herself to the evening's loneliness and start to cook supper. While she slaved in the kitchen, Martin stayed in his office sipping his red, red, wine.

"Martin," she called. No answer the first time.

"Martin," Mama called the second time, but still no answer. She had to call his name at least three times before father would respond.

"Martin!"

Then up from his chair he arose like a god descending his throne to stagger into the kitchen to meet Mama and me sitting at the table. Seething inside, we waited for him so that we could start eating Mama's Southern cooking—especially those to-die-for fried green tomatoes. When he came to supper, he sat, he ate, and when he was finished, he pushed his chair away from the table and wobbled back to his office where his lover "alcohol" awaited his return. Then, Mama and I (not even finished with our food) were left sitting at the table all by our lonesome. Every Martinless, fatherless night.

This lack of emotional connection with the man she married would upon occasion drive Mama into intense late night crying jags. Her tears tugged at my heart and I felt moved to sit quietly beside her and offer consolation to this poor woman because no matter what she did, she could not make a loving husband out of her self-absorbed housemate.

When Mama's crying subsided, we'd move from the couch in the living room back to the kitchen table where we drank cup after cup of Maxwell House coffee and pored over her relationship with her drunken spouse—her own cup of sorrows. If that old wooden table could talk, it would tell all about Mama's marriage to my father that felt to her like a merciless prison sentence from a cruel God who would neither heal nor kill the man who had become her captor. My Father's absolute preoccupation with self deeply wounded Mama, and she struggled to act like a strong Christian woman while living with this deeply troubled man.

I struggled, too.

When I was a little girl, I used to wait expectantly for father to come home from work each day. Near five o'clock, I'd put on my best frilly yellow polka-dotted dress, sit by the window and pray that God would change my father into the loving daddy I always wanted.

After an hour or so of my most sincere prayers, I'd see father's car coming down the street and into our driveway. Excitedly, I'd rush to the door to greet him hoping beyond hope that my prayers had been answered—that he'd walk through the door a changed man. "Daddy's home, my little princess," he'd say. And then he'd smile adoringly and cuddle me up in his arms.

But no matter how hard I prayed, this never happened. Day after day, the same old scenario repeated itself. He'd come home the same old person with the same old preoccupations. It didn't matter how excited, cute or needy I acted—he never gave me the loving response I wanted. If I tried to hug him, he'd push me away. If I tried to show him my report card, he'd tell me he was tired and would look at it after supper.

My attempts to connect with him seemed to irritate. What I wanted to talk about was silly. If I offered to fix his coffee, it wasn't hot enough. Bring him the paper? Couldn't do it fast enough. He was hard to please if he could be pleased at all. I knew it and Mama knew it, too. He related to her the same way.

I wish I could tell you differently, but that perfect father-daughter moment I longed for never happened. My attempts to win him over always failed. Every day that I lived with him, he gave me the same messages— "You are not worthy of my time and attention. You are a bother. You are not lovable and I wish you were never born."

Mama felt sorry for me because of his rejection and continually tried to make it up to me by buying clothes and toys. We could afford nice things on father's salary so I had anything a child could want—materially that is. But even my middle class privileges couldn't pacify the place in my heart that wanted a real relationship with my daddy. It seemed like all I would ever have was a phantom father three sheets to the wind with a house full of books. In my young mind, I thought perhaps I hadn't prayed hard enough or hadn't been good enough for God to answer my prayers.

Once, during one particularly depressing moment, it occurred to me that God might have been punishing me with this awful fatherlessness because I made fun of Thelma Lou Cratchett and her frequent rededications. So, thinking that both my heavenly and my earthly father were displeased with me, I began thinking that I would never be good enough for anybody. With this awful feeling stuck to me like glue, I began to hate myself because of my shortcomings.

And I certainly did not like my father because of his.

Chapter 4

Shame on us

If you are going to understand my father's weaknesses, you will have to understand the family he came from. Fleeing the great famine of the 1840s, Martin's ancestors came over on a boat to settle in the city of Boston. Uneducated, they all became beggars or common servants. Many worked as maids and butlers in the homes of well-to-do Bostonians whose relatives had come off the Mayflower in the 1600s.

These American elitists were not a welcoming bunch. They did not have the Southern hospitality mindset of Mama's people who would bake new neighbors a pie and tell them to "set a spell" as Granny Clampett on the "Beverly Hillbillies" would say. Oh, no! These uppity Northerners were proud, insolent people. Thinking more highly of themselves than they ought, they ridiculed and criticized their Irish servants for being dumb, drunken, quick-tempered and Catholic.

My father's father, Seamus, a ruddy, red-haired, freckled-face man, was the first in the family to overcome this servant mentality. He worked hard as a domestic for many years in a moneyed family in Boston and eventually saved enough to go to law school when he was a young man in his twenties. After graduating with honors, he vowed that his only child, Martin, would never be a low-life, working class fellow. To hear Martin tell it (and I only heard him tell it once when he was very drunk), Seamus, who once was employed by a tyrant, eventually became one. He demanded no less than perfection from his wife and child. Worth was performance. Performance was worth.

And since performance was the measuring stick, Seamus was going to make sure that he and his family were educated and performing well so that they could never be thought of as less-than-real Americans as his father and grandfather were. Sons of Shamus would never be victims of poverty, disease and Bostonian oppression. Taking this drivenness upon him, coupled with many years of sacrifice and hard work, Seamus had finally achieved his dream of making it in America. No son of his would achieve any less. No son of his would ever be called a "white nigger."

With his hard-earned title of attorney, Seamus was so noticeably proud of himself that he wanted his son to become a lawyer too. From the time my father was knee high to a duck he was encouraged, no—pressured, to follow in his father's footsteps and go to law school. And Martin, poor pitiful Martin, tried his best to fulfill his father's dreams, but without success.

He greatly disappointed Seamus one day when he came home and delivered the tragic news; he had flunked the bar exam. Not once, but twice. After these defeats, Martin tucked his tail between his legs and decided to become a college history professor. The next best thing, I guess. "Those who can, do; those who can't, teach," as the saying goes.

When Seamus realized that Martin would never be his law partner or the son he'd always wanted, the horrible shaming began. Every Christmas, when our family went back to Boston to visit Grandfather and Grandmother McBride, Mama and I had to endure father and son getting their Irish up over a failed exam that happened many moons ago.

"Martin?"

"What?"

"I thought you were never going to reply. You're as slow as a late supper," says Seamus.

"Give me a chance to finish my drink, before you start in on me," says my father.

"Martin. Did you ever think about perhaps talking that daughter of yours into going to law school when she grows up? Young ladies can do that nowadays ya know. Maybe she can make me a proud *man* since ya couldn't. Shame on ya, Martin, for being as lazy as a donkey with ya studies. Ya had the brains to make it if ya had tried harder, that is," said Seamus, with a tinge of an Irish accent he just couldn't hide. "Like I always say, 'Those who can, do. Those who can't, teach.'"

"Yes, and lawyers spend a great deal of their time shoveling smoke," my father retorted just for spite.

"What did ya say?" Seamus huffed.

"It's not what I said. It's what Oliver Wendell Holmes, Jr. said. Shall I repeat it?" My father snarled and tensed his lips when he spoke.

"What did I hear ya sayin', Martin? Are ya shamin' your own father? Ya think you're a smartarse do ya?"

"Smarter than lawyers like you who are classed in the natural history of monsters."

"Monsters? Are you sitting here in my house calling me a monster?"

And so it went. Back and forth. Just like this. Most of the visit. Between the Irish saying's and my mother's Southern saying's, which remarkably sounded just the same, I thought I would drown in a sea of irritating clichés.

There was shaming Seamus and there was *the wife*. Grandmother McBride was a pretty but passive woman who just sat by enduring the not so witty repartee and waiting for her husband to tell her what to do. Seamus had fallen in love with her, married her, and then molded her into a girl who could be ordered around and ignored. And the sorry thing was—she seemed to like it that way.

"Kathleen, get up. Get up *wife* and get me a cup of coffee and some for the family, ya hear? And bring some cakes while you're at it."

After hearing his crisp commands, into the kitchen she'd go to do his bidding, while Mama and I just looked at each other and rolled our eyes. My father tried this kind of shaming on Mama on a daily basis back home in Birmingham, but he did not get away with it for very long. After a minute or so of the demeaning talk, Mama would get up from her seat at the table, walk over to where father was sitting, dump his plate of food on his lap and simply walk away—a great dishonor for a man who had been raised by that shamer, Seamus.

Had Kathleen been from southern Ireland, perhaps she would have tried this, too. But because of that quick temper of her dear husband, she would have been slapped clear across the water, right back to the Noble Island. But, come to think of it, going back to the Noble Island might have been a good thing. Kathleen may have been happier with a common working class paddy who would have thought of her as his queen, instead of having to live with a shaming husband who thought she existed only to please him.

But as shame-based as father's family was—they didn't hold a candle to my Mama's kinfolk. Their shame didn't come from something as mild as being poor immigrants or having flunked a stupid bar exam. They had "serious shame"—as the evil-minded women at our yearly family reunion would say. The kind of humiliation that makes white trash out of respectable Caucasians. And I don't mean having relatives that live in a trailer with appliances sitting in their front yard.

So, let me quit beating around the bush and just spit it out.

My mother's Aunt's daughter's daughter, Darcy, did the dirty in the back seat of a Dodge with a black boy and conceived not one, but two mulatto children. Henry and Henrietta were their names—gorgeous babies with skin the color of coffee milk, always the talk at the reunions and the brunt of rude, racist comments.

"You'd better stay away from those pies until the grownups have eaten, or I'll spank your little black butts!"

"Oh, don't say stuff like that, Maylene," my great aunt Bessie chided, "They can't help it if they're black. They get in their drawers just like I get in mine. Don't you remember Pastor Peacock said we shouldn't be judging nobody—not *niggras*, drunkards, whores, cripples, re-tards, white trash *or* rednecks . . . and if he says not to judge. . . I ain't judging. I mean it Maylene—I ain't even judging the Jews who don't believe in, Jesus Christ—our white Savior".

Well, as they say, who did she think she was fooling? Certainly not me, even if I was just a kid back then. But in case you didn't put two and two together, I'll spell it out for you.

Bessie and Maylene were *racists*.

Nasty, evil, despicable racists. They came by it honestly. It was rumored that their Grandfathers, Bobby Earl and Cletus, were charter members of the KKK. I'm as serious as a heart attack. White hoods, masks, robes and all.

Truth be told, I was afraid of those women and I made it a point to stay as far away from them at the reunion as possible. Maylene and Bessie might have been giving folks the impression that that they had a soft spot in their hearts for *"the niggras"* as they pronounced it, but I knew the truth.

If they had known that I did more than rub shoulders with a black person they would have pitched a fit.

If you think I am telling you something about my Mama's side of the family that is too harsh, maybe a gentle cultural reminder will be helpful: Maylene and Bessie were born and raised in Birmingham, Alabama. *Birmingham*—the city that became a center for the civil rights struggle.

Maylene and Bessie grew up smack-dab in the heat of those issues and obviously didn't learn a darn thing. This is why I never told them that I had a black friend when I was in grade school. If perchance they *had* heard through the grapevine about my relationship with a black person, and would have caught me alone somewhere, they would have beaten me until I turned black *and* blue.

My friend's name was Kizzie. Kizzie Lewis. I met her in homeroom the first day of school when I was about eight or so. One week we were paired off by the P.E. teacher as tag team partners, and after that brief connection, we liked each other so much that we became best friends for the rest of grade school and on into junior high. We were inseparable. Swapped sandwiches at lunch. Passed notes in class. And once, when no one was looking, we pricked our thumbs and became blood sisters.

"You need to be mindful of a few things about them colored folk," Maylene used to say. "I know that the *niggras* get in their drawers just like I get in mine, but *honey child*, we *all* know that the good Lord didn't mean for the races to mix. *Whites* need to keep with the *Whites* and *Blacks* need to keep with the *Blacks*. Whites certainly shouldn't be bedding up with them like Darcy Ann did. It will lower their reputation, bring shame on their family."

When that crazy woman started talking like that, I'd be furious. The Lord didn't mean for the races to mix? So, there is going to be segregation in Heaven? St. Peter meets us at the Pearly Gates and says, "Blacks to the left, Whites to the right," as if he were sorting laundry? I don't think so.

Lord, have mercy on us. You couldn't run from it. You couldn't wish it away. Shame was everywhere in our family. Not just in Seamus. It was in us all—infusing our family with dishonor, condemnation and guilt. And with everyone feeling so badly about themselves so much of the time, it's a wonder we didn't kill each other.

In a way we did. Emotionally, that is.

Shame on us.

Chapter 5

The Shit List
(And Southern Baptist Jesus)

As they say in the South, my family was nothing short of a "hot mess." And because of this, I was the prime target for all those shaming religious devils intent on driving me to destruction. Going back to that that horrible day when I got saved and heard that terrifying sermon about the angry God, I somehow interpreted it, in my childlike mind, to mean that God was speaking through the preacher to let me know that He was personally out to get me.

And logic had it, if God was out to get me, I could only expect bad things to happen because He was after all a very mean God who delighted in sending people to…you know—H-E-Double-L. To the lake of fire and brimstone. To the pit of darkness. To eternal punishment where the worm does not die.

What do you think? Did that minister make a lasting impression on me, or not?

And so, with thoughts of Hell and the displeasure of the angry God (Southern Baptist Jesus) filling my mind most of the time, I was what some Southern women call—a mental case. Consumed by fear, anxiety and threat of God's punishment, I had to do something to silence the guilt I felt on a daily basis.

But, what? What would a little girl do to fix a big spiritual problem like this? Oh, what could I do to appease that demanding redneck God?

Then, one day, when I'd had just about enough of the demons beating their black wings against the portals of my mind, I came up with an idea. In an effort to keep those shaming devils at bay, I sat down at the kitchen table and wrote what I called "The List."

It went like this:

"The List"

1) Recite the Ten Commandments
2) Confess my sins up-to-date
3) Pray to keep dirty, wicked sinners out of Hell

And so, at the tender age of twelve, I recited, confessed and prayed every morning to silence the voices of Hell and please God. After a month or so of this ritual, I was beginning to feel better and more assured that I was on God's good side and had His favor. At last, there was something this church girl could do to quiet down the tormenting, condemning voices. "Surely God was seeing how serious I was about trying to be good and was rewarding my efforts when I did my list," I thought.

As long as I performed this ritual precisely—every day, come rain or shine, my worries about going to Hell and my feelings of shame stayed on the back burner. Oh, what a relief to this tormented soul! It was almost too good to be true. All I had to do to feel like a good church girl was to do my little list, and poof— fear and shame were all gone.

Finding something that worked this well, I knew I couldn't keep this discovery to myself. This wonderful technique had to be shared. So, one day when Mama and I were talking about the latest sermon our pastor preached called, "Do You Measure up to God's Standards?" I told her that I was quite certain that I did not and that in an effort to do better, I had created a list. Yes, this obsessive, compulsive church girl had written out a list that was keeping me on the straight and narrow and hopefully earning lots of brownie points for me from Father God and His angry, demanding son, Southern Baptist Jesus.

When she saw my list, she became excited and hoped a list like mine would work for her too. Completely in awe of my diligent efforts, Mama created a list of her own to add to her morning devotions. And so, thereafter (faithful and true) both of us church girls could be seen at the kitchen table—reciting, confessing and praying before we started our day.

If our day went well, we were sure that we had pleased God and purged our shame with our flawless performance of the list. If it didn't—well, we just knuckled down on our will power and tried harder. The ease of our lives (or lack thereof) was always related back to the list. Soon, yes, very soon after we started the performance, our self-righteous little "To Do" list had become for us the measure of our spirituality—the instrument that would sooth the savage shame within and keep Southern Baptist Jesus from sending us to… you know, H-E-Double-L.

But, just as we had hunkered down and gotten comfortable with our list, and were feeling so unique and spiritual, we found out (much to our dismay) that we weren't the only ones with spiritual "To Do" lists after all. At the weekly Community Bible Study Mama attended, there were plenty of Christians out there with lists. Bigger lists. Smaller lists. Wider lists. Taller lists. Believe it or not, there were some church girls who had their lists written on perfume-scented stationery that smelled like frankincense and myrrh. And, of course, those women who thought that they had the perfect lists were more than willing to make commentary on the lists that they deemed inferior.

Take for instance Minnie Maser, one of the seasoned church girls, who, when seeing Mama's list, rebuked her sternly and told her in no uncertain terms that "in order to be a good Christian your list needs to look more like this. . .

1. Send your extra change to your favorite missionary
2. Memorize the books of the Bible
3. Do nursery duty for the next month."

And then, when another woman, Betty Jane, overheard Minnie rebuking Mama about her list, she butted into their conversation uninvited and whipped out her own list and said, "Oh no, this ain't the right list. Your list ought to look like this. . . .

1. Send money to the starving children in Africa
2. Send letters of encouragement to the fat people in Weight Watchers

3. Send a case of Weight-off to Cousin Cassie who needs to lose 10 pounds before her senior prom."

And so it went around the room, just like that, with all of the women sharing their version of the correct list and criticizing each other's relationship with God when their friends' list didn't match their own.

So, by the time Mama came home from the bible study she was in tears. Sobbing her eyes out. "They told me that my list wasn't worth the paper it was written on," she whined. "They told me God required more of us than what is on our paltry little list. They told me that I needed to be spending more time in prayer and praise and scripture memorization. But, to tell the truth, I feel worn out just thinking about being a Christian. If I take all of their suggestions, we will never get out of this house and be able to get on about our day or go shopping or get a manicure or nothing. We'll be here working to please God until two o'clock in the afternoon. Shit, shit, shit on these lists!"

Anything that would drive Mama to cussing couldn't be good. She hated cussing. So, when I heard the "s" word roll from her lips like some common, white-trash whore, I knew that the list was bad news.

After the day that the women compared lists, Mama became even more committed to her spiritual disciplines than ever before. She didn't stop at that one list. She made others. One for Bible reading. One for praying. One for fasting. One for scripture memorization, etcetera, etcetera. And this is how she, no, how *we* lived our lives for the next few years. Making our lists. Checking them twice. But, instead of becoming sweeter and more Christ-like by doing all of those works, we both ended up being wound up tighter than an eight-day clock.

But one day Mama's severe self-discipline broke down. As a matter of fact, the worn out and haggard woman came to me like a Catholic going to her confessor. She told me to grab myself a cup of hot chocolate from the kitchen and come sit at the table because she had something that she wanted to tell me.

Eagerly, I did as she asked and sat myself down and locked eyeballs with her. Was there a new item to add to the list, I wondered?

"Maggie," she began hesitantly, "I have to get something off my chest."

"Ok, Mama, I'm listening."

"Maggie?"

"Yes, Mama?"

"Just for the record, I want you to know that I hate this damn list. I hate it. Hate it. Hate it! I feel like I'm dying and can't breathe. I feel like I'm bound in chains and can't move. I feel like I'm a slave and that God is a cruel taskmaster. If this is what it takes to make God happy, I guess He's just going to have to be mad. I can't take this anymore. I'm exhausted. Worn out as an old rocking chair. I am just so tired of trying to measure up."

"But, Mama," I said sympathetically, "maybe you just need a little break. God might get ticked off if we abandon this altogether. You know what they told us at church, that faith without works is dead. If we quit completely, you never know what might happen to us. Have you read the Old Testament, like Pastor told us to?"

"Yes, dear, I've read the Old Testament five times," she said, patronizingly.

"Then you know what God is capable of. If we don't keep up with our list, He might just send a plague or strike us dead or something worse. God was very unpredictable in that Old Testament," I said. "In my opinion, He was kinda like Father; you could never tell what was going to tick Him off. I read one page and He loves the Israelites, I turn the page and He hates them. On the next page he is healing them, on the next, killing them. Do what you want, Mama," I said, "but I wouldn't risk not doing the list if I were you. You need to beware of the wrath of God."

"Well, Shugah" (she called me "Shugah), "I guess you have a point," she said. "I need the wrath of God like I need a hole in my head."

Now, to any spiritually healthy person, the thought of having a list designed to keep your guilt and shame at bay would seem ridiculous. But, to me, after I'd heard sermon after sermon by Pastor Smith, with titles such as "You'd Better Watch Out" and "God can Read Your Evil Mind," the whole concept of the "all-knowing God" made me just a tad paranoid. Well, more than just a tad paranoid. Let me be honest with you—neurotic is more like it.

Sometimes at night, when I was about to fall asleep, I'd remember some unkind word I'd spoken to Mama or a kid at school who had made me mad. Then, I'd scarcely sleep a wink worrying that God was up in

Heaven making His big black marks in His big black Heavenly grade book which would all come back to haunt me on the big black Judgment Day.

I was scared to death that God and His strict son, Southern Baptist Jesus, would set some catastrophe in motion to chastise me for my sins. I stayed up apologizing to them half the night for things I had done and things I had left undone and promised them that if they would forgive me that I would *never* sin again. But, I (having a big mouth much like my mama's) couldn't keep my resolve for long. Just when I thought I had my tongue under control, something would happen to tick me off and I was back in that familiar rut—sin, repent, sin, repent, sin. And sin some more.

The only thing that brought me any semblance of relief from this turmoil was getting up the next morning, doing the things on my list, and feeling that fleeting sense of peace that came from my religious performance.

Our hellfire-and-damnation preacher had done a number on me for sure. He'd set the course for my spiritual walk and instilled in me an inordinate fear of God.

What an awful thing to give to an innocent child who was so tender and impressionable. Don't you agree?

I didn't know it back then, but in the depths of my heart, in the place unknown even to me, I had taken offense against that preacher. Devilish offense as poisonous as the fear he preached. Because being a church girl or not, I had unknowingly put this man on my list, too.

But, not on the lists I've been talking about.

On my Shit List.

Chapter 6

If Mama Ain't Happy, Nobody's Happy

There's an old saying in the South you may have heard: "If mama ain't happy, nobody's happy." It made its way to cliché status because it's true. Women are the heart of the home and if the heart's broken then everything else falls to pain.

It was an understatement to say that my mama was an unhappy woman while she was married to my father. Being miserable, just like my father, she ended up managing her brokenness with mood-altering substances. As religious as Mama was, she broke down one year and enhanced the peace of God with the peace of pills.

This mood-altering enhancement was frowned upon by the church she attended because as all the church girls told her that if she had enough faith, she wouldn't have to rely on prescription drugs to solve her problems. The church girls at the church were full of helpful platitudes like this one and offered them to her on a regular basis whenever she'd call the prayer chain, which was frequent. Why? You already know the answer to that question.

Because she was living with an alcoholic—my father, the heathen.

Let me tell you something: heathen is a strong word used by most Baptist preachers when referring to unbelievers and by Southern Mamas when describing immoral young men who want to date their daughters. "Don't have nothing to do with Billy Joe! He was seen drinkin' at the bar last night—that heathen!" and "You'd better keep a watch over that heathen cousin of yours; he'll try to git in your pants!" or "Don't go datin' that Martin McBride, he don't even believe in God—that heathen!"

But, it was too late for my mama—she had already gotten herself into trouble by marrying my heathen father and was reaping the consequences. You would have had to have known my mama to understand why she'd marry an unbeliever. She was attracted to people with problems—drawn to the afflicted, addicted and the heathen. If they were struggling, weak, or godless they won her heart.

So, my father fell into the godless-addicted category and won her heart in just three short months as they exchanged conversation about their respective worldviews over coffee and glazed doughnuts in the history department break room. Love slipped up on her while evangelizing the lost soul of Martin McBride.

Some Christians call this missionary dating. That is, when a woman tells herself she is only spending time with a man because she wants to win him to Jesus. Then she marries him because she is certain that in a short period of time he will believe the gospel and the power of her love will transform him into a wonderful person. Mama offered this reasoning up to God when she prayed about whether or not she should marry my father. She told God what she was going to do and prayed for Him to bless her decision. She obviously didn't believe what God said in the Bible about believers marrying heathen and found out after she said "I do" that she had made a horrible mistake and that she had thrown her college education down the toilet.

Having faith in God had always been difficult for Mama even though she was a church girl. Not loving God, but having faith in Him. Mama came from generations of faithlessness. Those who had a form of godliness but denied the power of God. Those who read the Bible and did what they wanted to do anyway. Those who eventually felt like they had to turn to pills to manage their dull, depressing lives.

So, in an effort to cope with her trying circumstances, Mama went on prescription drugs after my father's fortieth birthday party. That was the year she realized that she was married to an adulterer who was having an affair with himself, his liquor, his books and—and as Mama found out the night of his surprise party… with his secretary Ellen Dare.

Can you believe it? My boring, remote, drunken father was committing adultery with his secretary. It was so tacky, so cheap and so unoriginal. To make matters worse, the woman was ugly. And God don't like ugly. Ellen had horrible skin with moles all over her face and pudgy asymmetrical features that only served to accentuate her big, stained, horsy teeth.

She was a walking eye sore—that hussy whose name was penciled in my father's Day-Timer. And right next to her name was their whereabouts—119 Bella Vista Inn. Was my father dumber than a rock? Or did he want my mother to find out he was having an affair?

And find out, she did—at the most inopportune time. While she and the party guests were waiting for Martin to burst through the door so that they could yell, "surprise" and begin the celebration, Mama's intuition started talking to her. It told her that something wasn't right. And surprisingly, instead of tuning out that voice this time, Mama listened. At just the right moment when the guests were entertaining each other, she excused herself, went into Martin's office, opened father's Day-Timer, and there it was—the reason Martin was late to his own surprise birthday party.

He was shacked up in a motel room with Ellen Dare.

Surprise! Surprise!

Obviously, there was a secret hidden part of my father's life that Mama hadn't known about.

And here's the kicker—poor foolish Mama was the one who recommended that Father hire the home wrecker! She never thought that Ellen would be competition because she looked like she fell out of the ugly tree and hit every branch on the way down. But, as we all know, Mama was dead wrong. My father obviously saw something in that woman that was more than skin deep.

And so, immediately after seeing Ellen's name and the motel number written in the Day-Timer, Mama called the motel and was transferred to room number 119. Can you guess who answered? Martin? No, try again. Ugly Ellen who recognized Mama's voice and then hung up the phone before my incensed mother could even do a tell-off!

So there was Mama—stuck back in my father's office, hands shaking like a leaf, heart as traumatized and broken as can be, with a house full of supper guests. But, instead of doing what she wanted to do (which was crawl into a hole and die), she collected herself and walked back into the dining room to as if the revelation of adultery had never happened.

Around eight o'clock, when the crowd had finished the last of the mixed nuts, Martin—that low down traitor, walked into the living room where thirty impatient people were waiting to help him celebrate his fortieth birthday. Not an emotional person, he barely reacted when in unison his colleagues shouted "surprise," but when he saw food on the table—now that brought a smile to his face. Mama had slaved all afternoon making his favorite traditional Southern meal: fried chicken, black-eyed peas, turnip greens, creamed potatoes, cornbread, sweet tea and blackberry cobbler. And since he had previously been rumbling with Ellen, he had an enormous appetite. So, in spite of his shameful actions—the hungry heathen decided to enjoy the party.

At first Mama tried to pretend that nothing was wrong. Like a proper church girl, she even offered up a proper blessing before supper. I was amazed that she could pray, considering.

> *God is great; God is good, now we thank Him for our food.*
> *By His hands, we all are blessed. Come, Lord Jesus, be our guest...*
> *In Jesus' name we pray,*
> *Amen.*

During the prayer, Mama was flashing a look in Father's direction—and if looks could kill, he would be a dead man. But, he didn't see it. His lying eyes were closed. And not because he was *praying.* That sorry heathen was thinking about his last date with ugly Ellen, I supposed.

Well, before Mama could finish amen-ing, the folks were at the food like ravenous vultures. You should have seen those prissy professors' wives shed their Southern manners and go at that fried chicken. There wasn't a lowly gizzard left on the platter.

When the meal was finished, and the cobbler had added an extra pound to the hips of those weight conscious women, Mama folded her napkin, patted the last bit of pearly pink lipstick from her tense and angry mouth and excused herself from the table. Then, taking a few hesitant steps, she ran headlong into the bathroom and slammed the door so loudly I thought she was going to take it off the hinges.

From where I was sitting, I could hear her turning the water faucet on—as if a small stream of running water was going to mask her mournful sounds. Never before in my life had I heard such cries. Howlings so deep and guttural they chilled me to the bone.

But the curious thing about that outburst of pain was that it ended almost as soon as it had begun.

Before I could wrap my mind around what was happening, Mama burst out of the bathroom like a banshee yelling, "I have an announcement to make! I want to tell y'all why Martin was late to his own birthday party. He was shacked-up with his secretary Ellen Dare. Yes, folks, he's screwing around on his wife with his butt-ugly secretary—bless her heart."

And for your information, a Southern woman can say anything about anyone no matter how cutting or evil if she just follows it up with "bless her heart," or something similar like:

> *Don't go repeating this, but Mrs. Johnson's loose daughters, Babs and Lola, became porn whores—bless their hearts.*

> *Violet's thighs looked like a tub full of cottage cheese in that skimpy bathing suit—bless her heart.*

> *Mrs. Murphy's lusty cousins, Beebe and Hortence, are both living in sin—bless their hearts.*

I think you get the point.

So, anyway, Mama had a crack in her voice when she made that tawdry announcement about Ellen and I knew she was already ashamed of herself and afraid of Father's response at the same time. But, obviously, her pain and anger were at intolerable proportions for her to come unglued in public like that and taint her reputation as good church girl. She didn't act too ladylike.

Incensed, Martin flashed Mama a look I'd seen him give her a hundred times before—the one like angry demons peering out from behind his blue-green eyeballs. Then, (this is the best part), my father, all flustered in his tight-assed self, took one of Mama's china plates off the table and hurled it in her direction, barely missing her newly shampooed and styled sausage curls. Embarrassed and humiliated, he stomped out of the room like a two-year-old having a tantrum and went straightway into his office. And me—I just stood over in the corner watching it all, wishing that I were anywhere but home.

Since his high-minded colleagues had never seen this angry side of Martin, they just stood there holding their drinks in their hands like stunned statues. But after several minutes of pretending that they weren't witnessing the domestic quarrel, one poor soul finally got up the nerve to call it an evening and then he (along with twenty-nine others) exited our home in the most horrible silence I'd ever heard.

After the guests left, Mama sent me to my room. "Go to your room, Maggie. Your father and I are going to have a little talk," she said sternly. Well, I don't know about your Mama, but when mine said, "go to your room," it was the signal for trouble. Not daring to disobey at this critical moment, I did as she said, no questions asked.

But, since I couldn't stand not knowing what was going on, I pressed my head against the wall beside my bed at just the right angle so I could hear Mama and my father having it out in the hall.

I thought I was going to have a permanent crick in my neck the way I had to contort myself to hear them fight without actually opening my bedroom door. But after just a few minutes, their argument became unusually heated and I did not have to strain to hear anymore. Their muffled words soon exploded into a clear, terrifying brawl. I heard the sound of wood popping, followed by a heavy thud as my mother's slender body hit the floor.

Apparently, she said some things uncharacteristic for a church girl and father responded like an offended Irishman with physical force—the spirit of Seamus rising up in him. Mama had started in on him like she was not supposed to do, for she wasn't fortunate enough to have read any literature on how the wife of an alcoholic should behave. She didn't know that she was caught up in a transgenerational dynamic, a family disease, a cunning, baffling, and powerful illness. She wouldn't find that out until the 1980s. Back then, she didn't have a therapist to coach her on the right words to say at just the right time in order to keep his violent temper at bay. She had to wade through this mess all by herself.

And so, not thinking about the ramifications, raw and unrestrained, she opened her shaming mouth and reacted from her gut. She cursed him like a sailor for having an affair with that ugly Ellen woman. And Father, coming from scrapping Irish stock, didn't take to a woman getting up in his face and telling him anything. One can only imagine what that abusive man did to give that woman a black eye, broken ribs and a bloody nose.

When the fighting had stopped and Mama was lying alone in the hall all bruised and bloody, her mind began to wander down that bitter memory lane. It made her sick to her stomach thinking about all the nights she played second fiddle to the bottle and the books. It made her head ache pondering all the evenings she spent as a married widow in solitude and silence. And then, with all of those bad memories fueling her anger again, she got a second wind. In an instant, she pulled her mad self off the floor and ran into the office where Martin was pouring himself a drink. Catching him by surprise, she lunged in his direction and clawed the man's lying eyes out!

Acting like a she-devil, that slender church girl tore into him like a lion. She called him every name in the book just like a stark raving lunatic. Then, after she had her say, she ran into the bathroom, but failed to shut the door. Plopping herself down on the toilet, she put her face in her hands and cried. But, Mama was not crying tears just for this awful birthday party and her failed marriage, no—she was crying tears for her whole unhappy life. Her whole, lonely, loveless life that was greatly intensified when she married my father. Martin was supposed to have been the one to make up for the lack of love in her life. He was supposed to fill the empty places in her heart that her own father created. But, sorrowfully, he did not. He just made the empty places emptier like a cold dark well.

Tired of fighting and tired of crying, Mama got off the toilet and stared at her wounds in the mirror. Not knowing that I was sneaking around, I watched her from the hall as she saw for the first time, the damage my father had done to her body. Cuts. Bruises. Visible wounds, there for all to see. But, as hurtful as these were, they were nothing compared to the invisible ones —the agonizing ache in her heart from betrayal and rejection by the man she loved.

From this day forward, Mama was one unhappy woman. Consequently, I was one very unhappy child, because if you people haven't figured it out by now—

"If Mama ain't happy, nobody's happy."

Chapter 7

Coven Women

THE FEELINGS I FELT THAT day knowing that my family was going to hell in a handbag were more than I could stand. Betrayal. Adultery. Domestic Violence. Big issues for such a little girl. It didn't seem fair. I had just gotten saved from Hell and now I was living in Hell. Although it had been less than three months since I walked the aisle and became a church girl, the night I heard my father beat my mother I cursed God for letting me be born the daughter of that mean Martin McBride.

I wish I could tell you differently, but there wasn't a happy ending to this story. No kiss and make up scenes between my parents. No cease-fire. No reconciliation. Three weeks after the revelation of Martin's adultery, Mama got fed up with seeing lipstick on his collar and demanded that Martin leave Ellen once and for all or pack his bags and get the hell out.

But, Martin, not wanting to leave Ellen (or get the hell out), told Mama in no uncertain terms that he would never leave his house; the one he paid for with his hard-earned money. He also told her that unless she wanted to be sharing a home with his mistress, she would have to go. Well, there was no way in hell that Mama was going to live with that ugly Ellen woman.

So we went.

We packed up our hurt, pain, rejection and unforgiveness in a set of American Tourister luggage and walked out on that sorry Martin McBride. In hindsight, Mama's ultimatum really wasn't an ultimatum at all. It was nothing but a drastic measure from a woman who was hoping that her marriage could be saved if she were to stand by her Christian principles and put her foot down.

Divorce wasn't what Mama wanted. What she wanted was for her husband to come to his senses. Most of all, she wanted him to miss her desperately, bring her flowers and beg for her forgiveness. But from what I've told you about the man, you can see that the chances of this happening were slim to none. Martin didn't share her values about marriage. He wasn't accountable to God, to Mama or to anybody else for that matter.

Mama was devastated about the breakup of the relationship, but not Martin. He took the departure of his wife and child the way he took everything else—dispassionately. I think that he was relieved not to have us always reminding him that he was a selfish self-centered son-of-a. . . Seamus.

You were hoping I was gonna say it, weren't you?

And so, like it or not, Martin's life went on without us just fine and we had to make the best of it.

The judge who presided over the divorce awarded alimony to Mama. With that extra money, she bought a lovely three-bedroom house just a mile away from our former home. A great decorator, she furnished it tastefully and promised she'd buy a new bedroom suite for me if only I would quit whining about losing the father I really never had. Enticed by her offer, I stuffed my pain and picked out a brand new white wicker bed, dresser and a pair of matching nightstands. After the deliverymen arranged the furniture in my bedroom, I knelt down beside my brand new purchase and thanked God not only for the furniture but that the furniture was in a house and not in a trailer. To live in a trailer, by gosh, was to admit to the world that you were of the blue-collar class. And Mama, having gotten used to her privileged position as a professor's wife, would not stand for that. And neither would I. While living with Martin and Careen, I had acquired a moderate amount of snobbery. Not enough to send me to Hell, but just enough to be class-conscious.

Anyway, after the delivery, set up and the prayer, I stood alone in my room admiring my furniture and vowing that a messed up man would never hurt me again. A tear ran down my face when I thought about my father but I quickly wiped it away. I had to face the facts. Pull myself up by my bootstraps.

My father was gone. It was all over but the shouting.

But, while I was stuffing my pain, Mama was busy feeling hers. She cried for days. She cried for nights. For five weeks straight, she cried every morning while she was in the shower getting ready for work. Not even the sounds of gallons of water pouring from the nozzle could mask the sound of her gut wrenching, grief-filled cries.

She thought I couldn't hear her cry while she was bathing, but I could. And what I heard was beyond pitiful. I had never felt so sorry for anyone in my life. After these intense emotional releases, she would pull herself together, dress, come down for breakfast and tell me for the gazillionth time that it was just a matter of time before Martin realized what he had lost and come to his senses.

Then, while I was finishing my cereal, I listened to her pie-in-the-sky hopes as best I could without getting angry. But, sometimes, when I had just about enough of it, I had to stop myself from reaching across the breakfast table and slapping her into the middle of next week. My father was gone and he wasn't coming back. Couldn't she get it through her thick head? She was a woman scorned and a soon to be divorcée who would bear the stigma of that status in the church world. How could I see this and a grown woman couldn't?

Meanwhile, with Mama still in lala land, months went by without any communication from Father except for envelopes he left in our mailbox that contained money and notes about his travel schedule in case of an emergency. Each time she retrieved the mail, she dug into those letters as if she were on the verge of getting that much awaited "I still love you, I'm coming home" message. But each and every time she opened the envelope, she was sorely disappointed. There was nothing else in there besides money and a schedule. Nothing. No promises to reconcile. No words about weekend visitations with his daughter. Nothing. Father had made a new life for himself and it didn't include us.

One day while Mama was sitting on the front porch swinging while drinking a glass of sweet tea so lost in the fantasy that Martin would change in due time because of prayer and love, she happened to notice her neighbor who was walking her sassy "Shih-tzu"—excuse the cuss word.

They met, talked, and before you knew it—Mama was pouring her heart out about her marital problems to her newfound friend.

And it just so happened that this new friend, Francis, was attending a prayer group at The Covenant Legalists Church, a peculiar form of Legalism. Luckily, it was just a few blocks away from our Baptist church and five other houses of worship that were all lined up in a row on the same street. Anyhow, this group of Legalists women formed their group so that they could get together and pray in hopes that God would restore their marriages. So, pitiable in her grief, Mama got all excited at the prospect that she could pray her sinful spouse back into her life. Not wanting to waste any time, she immediately ditched the Baptists and hooked up with the Covenant Legalists. Before the week was over, she was a member of the group called, "Covenant Ladies." Francis was the group's co-leader.

Today, when I tell this story, I jokingly call the group "*Coven Ladies*" because the gals sat around in a circle chanting:

> "He's coming home in Jesus' name,
> I call him back from sin and shame.
> God hates divorce; it breaks His heart.
> We'll stick it out till death we part!"

I figured that their little group was just going to chant their legalistic, broken hearts out until their husbands left their mistresses and came to their senses. Those she-devils were going to exert the power of their will to make it happen. Francis assured Mama of Martin's speedy return home if Mama would only pray hard enough. Francis also reminded Mama about the wedding vows: "Wherefore they are no more twain, but one flesh. What therefore God hath joined together, let not man put asunder." Or woman. In this case—Ellen. Butt-ugly Ellen.

But let me ask you this: "Did God join Martin and Careen McBride?" Everyone who has ever read the Bible knows that God doesn't join believers with heathen. The churchwomen, above all people, should have known this. Looking back on it, I wish I had given them a piece of my mind. What they didn't count on was their "Covenant" doctrine turning my Mama into an obsessive, compulsive prayer addict. On any given night, I could walk by Mama's bedroom and see her down on her knees praying for hours—praying and hoping and begging and pleading. I got tired of hearing all of it. And I'd bet my last dollar that God did too.

If those witchy women had lived inside my home for just one day, they could have seen that Mama and Martin were in no way joined together. They were as twain as twain could be while they were still married. Those women belonged in a coven not a church. They might as well have put on some black pointy hats and gathered about a caldron with a bottle of herbs and eye of newt while they prayed. They were exerting so much pressure on Mama to produce "The Return of Martin McBride," that she almost had a nervous breakdown.

The women had so bought into the covenant doctrine that they didn't even stop to think that maybe Jesus didn't want my Mama to live with a man given over to addiction, adultery and violence. And that maybe—just maybe, divorce was the compassionate way of escape that God made so that women like Mama could get on with their lives.

Some women (in an effort to convince the wandering spouse that God was going to make them return home), wrote threatening scriptures on their husbands' car windows. Were these women blooming idiots? What were the odds that any self-respecting man would respond favorably to the "turn or burn" approach to reconciliation? Didn't romantic suppers, and negligees, cross their minds? Or were they so heavenly minded that they were no earthly good? Nonetheless, Mama overlooked their cultish ways and faithfully attended the weird group, chanting and praying with the best of them. All the while, Martin was not turning, nor burning, but continuing his adulterous lifestyle feeling another type of fire. The fire of lust.

After a whole year of this wicked witchcraft crap and while Martin had yet to express any interest in reconciliation, Mama finally began to realize that the Almighty was not going to make Martin McBride do anything. Although it says in the Bible that the "fervent prayers of righteous persons avail much," it soon became evident that there was something called free will involved. That wonderful power of choice that God gave to everyone.

Martin was going to remain a heathen as long as he chose to be a heathen and that was that.

And this dose of grim reality made Mama sadder than ever before.

CHAPTER 8

NICE WHITE MICE

ALTHOUGH MAMA WAS DISILLUSIONED WITH the crazy "Coven Ladies" and their theology about marital reconciliation, she decided not to forsake the Legalists altogether and offer her services as a pianist. The sisters in the group informed her that the full-time piano player had resigned and would be leaving in just a matter of days.

After hearing about this opportunity, Mama went home, dragged out her old hymnbooks, honed her skills, and got up the nerve to call the minister and ask about the pianist position. Full of anticipation, her bubble burst when the Reverend Nigel Stogging refused to let her apply. As anal as they come, he cited the strict church rules that stated, "Each person in the music ministry of Covenant Legalists has to be a member in good standing for at least one year before he or she could be considered for a staff position at the church."

During that year, the poor congregant would have time to prove that they were a person worthy of being called a Christian. Jump through the religious hoops. Attend church every time the doors were open. Lead a small group meeting. Cook for Wednesday night suppers. Give tithes and offerings. Blah, blah, blah, blah, blah.

After hearing just another religious "to do" list, Mama took issue with the rule in a clever way by rubbing the Reverend's nose in a scripture from the book of James: "Religion that is pure and undefiled before God, the Father, is to visit orphans and widows in their affliction, and to keep oneself unstained from the world." After laying this guilt trip on him, Mama says that the Reverend Stogging just stood there with his mouth wide open as if he were catching flies.

And seeing that a little guilt was working on him, she figured that more would work even better so she laid it on even thicker: "People should be ashamed of themselves for not thinking of the less fortunate. It is the church's duty to help take care of widows and orphans, Reverend, is it not?"

But before he could answer, Mama added, "In principle, Reverend, my daughter and I are an orphan and a widow. My husband abandoned us. He committed adultery and ran off with his butt-ugly secretary—bless her heart. I'm sure you know, Reverend, that in the Old Testament, all it took for a child to be an orphan was to be without a father. And my poor, dear girl, Maggie—is without a father. He doesn't call. He doesn't write. He doesn't see her at all. So Biblically speaking—she's an orphan. Fatherless. But I'm not telling you anything that a handsome, intellectual man like you doesn't already know, am I?"

It was a pretty good argument for a woman who'd never been to Bible school, if I do say so myself. And pretty good flattery thrown in there, too. Either because of God or because of her persuasive power, her small sermonette must have touched a place in the minister's stony heart. He scratched his head, thought for a minute and then changed his mind. That rigid man of the cloth actually bent the rules and allowed Mama to audition for the job. And being the incredible piano player that she was, Mama dazzled him and was hired right on the spot.

Rejoicing in the good news, she came home glowing and took me to town with her to pick out some new Sunday clothes. It had been a long time since we had gone shopping together and I was so looking forward to spending time with Mama. During our shopping excursions we usually listened to our favorite songs on the radio, played "I spy," grabbed a bite of lunch and talked about anything and everything that came to mind.

Our favorite place to eat was the Woolworth's store. I loved the smells—the buttery popcorn, the cotton candy and the greasy hamburgers frying on the grill. It was magical being in that charming five and dime. Once inside, we made a beeline to our special place; the counter with the red vinyl stools. Hungry and impatient, we watched as the grey-haired grannies served up a big platter of crinkle fries with Heinz ketchup. My favorite.

During these special times that Mama and I spent together, she'd start into her storytelling. I can see and hear her even now, in that flowery way she used to express herself, sitting all dressed up on that fancy stool with her long, slender legs crossed and one foot just a swinging. "Did I ever tell you about the time my selfish sister left after Big Daddy shot a bobcat?" she'd say.

"Yes, Mama, you did," I said. But that didn't stop her from telling it again. Usually her endless repetition really got my goat, but not when we were at the Woolworth's store. So what if I'd heard the story a thousand times before—we were in my favorite five and dime. Not about to make a fuss, I nodded my head and smiled as if to say, "Let's hear it again." Already as talkative as a Chatty Cathy wind-up doll, Mama channeled that energy into her storytelling.

"Yeah, one day Big Daddy decides that he's going hunting," she began. "So, he grabs his shotgun and heads out to the front porch to put on his hunting shoes that he had placed on the mat by the door. Not paying much attention, he bends down to pick them up and—*Honey child*, you don't even want to know. A stray bobcat, sitting nearby, had messed in his one and only pair of hunting shoes. Being the man that he was—he was not going to stand for that. He was going to show that cat who was boss. In a rage, he walked toward the varmint, cocked his shotgun and blew the poor bobcat's brains out. And this, *Shugah*, was the reason my baby sister Justine ran away from home when she was sixteen. She said she just couldn't take his anger anymore. That selfish girl, always thinking first of number one, packed her bags and went traipsing off with her boyfriend while I was left at home to live in H-E-Double L."

Although I had heard that story a million times before, I listened as if it were the first. And I assure you, it wasn't the last. I heard it again the following week. And the week after that. As sure as the sun rose in the East, Mama never tired of rehearsing childhood drama, especially when they involved her sister Justine.

Mama would have skinned me alive if she had ever known I said it, but Mama was jealous of Justine. *Jealous.* And not without a good reason. Mary Justine Monroe looked like an aristocratic 1940's movie star—admired for her charm and sophistication wherever she went. Unlike Mama, Justine had married Christian and married rich. Her husband, Frank Monroe, a well-known cardiologist, made more money than the law would allow. Hard working and faithful, he kept Justine in the style she had become accustomed to in their high-class home in Mountain Brook, the richest city in Alabama. Ironically, her doting husband died from a heart attack. Although she missed him terribly, her sadness was greatly diminished by the multi-million dollar life insurance policy he left to her when he passed away *and* by Rico the gardener—but those are family secrets that this church girl *won't* talk about.

Because of Mama's deep and chronic resentments about the huge financial gap between her and her sister, I hadn't seen Aunt Justine for a long time. But, if there was one thing I learned while growing up in the McBride family, it was to know when to keep my mouth shut and this was one of those times. I knew better than to talk about Justine after Mama's belabored story of her selfish sister leaving her to live in Hell while she went traipsing off with her boyfriend. Because, in spite of what Jesus taught about forgiveness, Mama had been holding a grudge against her sister ever since they had their falling out after my Grandmother's funeral—which is a doozy of a tale itself.

But before that rift, before that hideous funeral (a story I'll save for later), Aunt Justine and I were like two peas in a pod. When Mama allowed me to visit her, we loved spending time at the place she loved the most— The Club. My pretty and fascinating Aunt sure showed me some good times back then. She was rolling in dough and spent money like it grew on trees. And in spite of the ugly undercurrents between Justine and Mama, the memories of those times were still dreamy and oh, so very special.

The Club was amazing. I thought I'd died and gone to hog heaven whenever my aunt took me to that place. With my head in the clouds and dollar signs in my eyes, I imagined that Justine and I were movie stars strolling through the place, staring longingly at the refined members with their old wealth sophistication. Although Justine was nouveau riche (which bugged the stew out of middle class Mama,) she wasn't stingy at all. Quite the opposite. Justine was generous and as free-hearted as they come. When it was suppertime at The Club, she'd buy me anything that I wanted and tell the waiter to put it on her tab.

After she ordered her usual lobster and escargot, she'd nod, smile, and hand me the menu. I'd grab it greedily and eye that thing like a dog after a bone. Then, in my most lady-like adult voice, I'd turn to the waiter and say, "I'll have the Chicken Cordon Bleu." Desperately trying to sound grown up, I said it clearly, quickly, and with just a hint of a French accent for show. When it was all said and done, I wasn't easy on my rich aunt's pocketbook. My bill alone came to over fifty dollars. But she didn't mind. And back in nineteen seventy-something that was a pretty penny.

When we were both full and happy, we'd go sit at the bar where my self-indulgent aunt would drink mint flavored martinis and smoke herself silly. A sight for sore eyes, I can still see her pucker her red lips and take long, slow drawls from the soothing cigarettes. Enviously, I watched her chiseled chin tilt upwards as to play tantalizingly with the billowing smoke rings. She was beautiful. Boastful. Betty Davis was written all over her. Then, when the lazy hours had slipped into evening, Justine would croon, "All good things have to come to an end. All good things have to come to an end."

And with that sad finale, the good things did come to an end. I watched her when she thought I was not looking. Watched her slowly and deliberately leave the bar and motion for the driver to get her jet black Mercedes. After that, not completely drunk, but not completely sober either, Justine would collect herself and drive me back to her house where we'd sit on the sofa and flip through Cosmopolitan magazines and play with her lap dogs—Molly and Millie. Summers with my Aunt Justine were lovely and, of course, passed much too quickly.

All because Justine lavished me with money and attention, I grew to love the woman. And this, *Honey Child* (as Mama used to say), was just one more thing that made my life difficult. In offering my affections to Aunt Justine, I was breaking the unspoken rule—You Don't Betray Mama. I was supposed to like who Mama liked and hate who she hated. If Mama hated blueberries, I hated blueberries. If she disliked the color orange, I disliked orange. If she hated Justine… I… well, you get the point.

Now, back to my story. In that awkward moment at the Woolworth's store, when Mama brought up Justine's name and the selfish sister story, I did what I usually did—I pretended not to hear and not to hurt. Instinctively, I did something that little peacemakers do. I grabbed Mama's hand and said, "Let's not think about sad things on our shopping trip today—let's think about happy things. Let's go buy some girly clothes and be the most beautiful women at church Sunday!"

Mama agreed and quickly placed her hand in mine as I began to sing, "I've got the joy, joy, joy, joy, down in my heart." As if singing about it would make it so. And then Mama sang, "Where?"

"Down in our hearts, Mama…down in our hearts," I reminded her. "Mama, you know the song so, sing it!"

Then, after we had amused absolutely no one but ourselves with our silliness, we headed outside to pound the pavement and look for bargains. Spending money that day seemed delicious and daring. We shopped for hours until the soles of our feet were aching so badly it felt like we would drop. When evening came and we were all worn out, but fully satisfied with all of our glorious purchases, we returned home with sacks full of clothes.

Mama said that she wanted to make a stunning impression at our first Sunday service when she made her debut as the new pianist.

"Let's try our new outfits on!" she exclaimed excitedly, as soon as we walked through the door. Dumping the contents of the sacks onto the couch, I picked out the new red dress she bought for me and headed to the bathroom to try it on. Then, she picked her favorite outfit—the black and white polka-dotted pants suit and headed toward the bedroom to change. When we met each other back in the living room, I couldn't believe how pretty she was with her slender figure. I was always so proud to be seen in public with Mama because she always looked like she had stepped out of a band box—a dead look-a-like for Grace Kelly.

After we had tried all of our new clothes, I put on a pot of coffee. Then, we sat in the living room for hours sipping on the strong brew and admiring each other in our snazzy frocks. Finally, after much coffee and conversation, we said our goodnights and went to bed. All in all, it was a very good day.

Before you knew it, Sunday morning rolled around and there we were—slap dab in the middle of a Legalist service and before you could say Pharisee! Proud to be there, Mama was radiant as she lifted those talented fingers off the keyboard, having just finished her first offertory. Then, after the thunderous applause Mama got from the congregation, the pastor of Covenant Legalist positioned himself to deliver the sermon.

Accenting his glowing countenance were the expensive vestments—the majestic robe and stole ensemble, brilliantly color-coordinated with the current season of the church year. With his commanding presence in the pulpit, Reverend Stogging wasted no time getting to the heart of his sermon.

His text was the second chapter of Acts concerning the day of Pentecost. Fairly dramatic for a Legalist, his quivering voice intensified in volume with each passing sentence during the oration. While the highly impressed congregants uttered repeated chants of "So be it" and "Amen," I'm sure that Stogging's idol, I. B. Natas, the founder of Legalism, looked down from the portals of Heaven and admired the careful way the minister was expounding on the outpouring of the Holy Spirit from the second chapter of Acts:

And when the day of Pentecost was fully come, they were all with one accord in one place. And suddenly, there came a sound from Heaven as of a rushing mighty wind, and it filled all the house where they were sitting…

During the preacher's sermon, I sat quietly (like a good church girl) on the piano bench beside Mama. Since I was helping Mama turn the pages in the hymnal, I was waiting for the sermon's climax when Mama would begin playing the closing hymn. But, in the midst of this holy moment, there came a great disturbance—rumbling sounds echoing from the storage closet located just to the right of the piano.

Hmm… "Mice. Nice white mice," I thought, in a Southern accent, of course.

Deciding to ignore the rumble and bring my wandering mind back to the sermon, I heard the preacher say something about the Upper Room and the Holy Ghost bursting on the scene with cloven tongues of fire…

"Darn, there's that sound again," I thought. Another distraction. More rumbling. The sound of paws and claws, scratching, coming nearer. I began to do some serious worrying. "What if a critter runs out from behind the door in the middle of his sermon?" What a crazy thought. It would never happen. My silly imagination!

The minister continued…

…And there appeared unto them cloven tongues like as of fire, and sat

upon each of them. And they were all filled with the Holy Ghost and began to speak with other tongues, as the Spirit gave them utterance.

But, before I could stop my imaginings, before I could calm my anxious mind, the unthinkable happened. I kid you not, two fat white mice dashed out from behind the door and leapt into my lap all panicky and agitated.

…and they began to speak with other tongues as the Spirit gave them utterance.

"Help me Jesus!" I shrieked loudly.

No sooner had I howled out the good Lord's name in vain that the pesky intruders scurried back into their hiding place in the storage room. At the same time, I caught a glance of the congregation. They had pinned themselves back against the pews and appeared as frightened cardboard figures all lined up neatly in a row. Then, in utmost terror, I glanced over to where the deacons sat. They all looked like the portraits you've seen of the early church fathers—Wesley, Calvin, Martin Luther—the somber, sour ones who had their pictures taken pre-Prozac. At this point, the Legalist minister blinked and turned his head 180 degrees, looking through Mama and directly at me like a devil set on fire and raging with the fury of Hell.

"Can you not control your child, Sister?" He called Mama "Sister."

"Oh, no, my Mama's gonna get canned," I thought! As for the congregation—you could have heard a pin drop.

Because of my reaction to the mice, Brother Stogging pulled Mama aside after the service was over and informed her, as I highly suspected he would, that he no longer needed her services.

Mama was fired.

The mice were poisoned.

But on the upside, we looked absolutely gorgeous leaving the Covenant Legalist Church.

CHAPTER 9

THE GREAT DEPRESSION

WELL, WHAT DO YA KNOW? Getting fired was the jolt Mama needed to end the other relationships in her life that weren't working. Two weeks after she lost her job, she also quit the Covenant Ladies and filed for divorce. As guilty as she felt about ending her marriage, she seemed strangely at peace and more than relieved to be out of that useless prayer group.

But, I should have known better. This was just the calm before the storm. After three short months of tranquility, things changed. All of a sudden, almost out of nowhere, Mama became disgruntled, withdrawn, and began to obsess about her age. "What man is going to want a forty year-old wrinkled woman with a preteen?" she'd whine.

So, for the next year Mama drove me to school in her pajamas, returning home only to crawl back into bed, pop her pills, and cry her middle-aged self back to sleep. In the afternoons, I rode the bus home. When I walked in the door Mama could still be found in her bedroom with the shades drawn, listening to the tear-jerking recording of "I Will Always Love You" by Dolly Parton. Many an evening I'd go into her bedroom, shut off the 8-track player and beg her to join me in the land of the living.

"Mama, get up out of the damn bed (this church girl had taken to cussing) and forget about that man! He's not worth it," I said, trying to convince myself of the same. Even though Mama vehemently protested, she'd eventually make her way to the kitchen, heat up a can of soup, eat, and return to bed. Most evenings Mama left me alone with a bowl of

Campbell's tomato soup and no company at all except for Spiegel the beagle. Interestingly, Spiegel was named after my favorite catalog.

Spiegel was a cute little brindle dog, full of vim and vigor. He was no substitute for Mama, but at least he was not in bed at four o'clock in the afternoon. Mama did a good thing by giving me the feisty pup as consolation for losing my father. While she was in bed, the dog kept me company. Not only was he lovable, but he was smart as a tack. Shook hands. Rolled over. Played dead. Fetched Mama's nerve pills. He was more valuable than a maid.

The talented dog and I became very close friends during Mama's depression. Late at night, having nothing better to do, I'd go sit on the back porch and pour out my heart to that pooch. God only knows—I told that critter almost everything including the fears that whispered darkness into my ears saying, "You've already lost your father, and now you are losing your mother, too. We've got you now," those demons jeered.

During this gloomy season, Mama was sad, tense, irritable and just plain hard to be around. She sat and stared at the floor for minutes on end. She refused to eat. She complained incessantly about her age. She did only what she absolutely had to do to make things hang together and keep up appearances—like going to the grocery store and taking me to school. If I came home from school with good news she'd stare straight though me and return to the dark night of her soul. She said that she not only felt forsaken by Martin, but by God, as well. It seemed to me she didn't even try to help herself. As Aunt Justine would say, "Some people just like having the poor mouth. If there ain't nothing to cry about, they'll crawl under the house just to get to say it's dark."

So, Mama was emotionally under the house and it sure was dark under there. It was like she had resigned from the land of the living. She didn't want to bathe, bake or talk to anyone. I knew that her depression was really serious when she stopped baking.

Mama had rather bake than breathe back in the day. It was her gift. Her passion. She was a natural-born baker who was known all over the county for her blueberry cobbler. "Here comes the "Cobbler Lady," the folks would say." Cross my heart and hope to die if that scrumptious dessert wouldn't have melted in your mouth and sent your taste buds to shivering. All the judges at the State Fair said so and gave her the first place ribbon every year for Careen's Cobbler. But sadly, there was no entry at the fair the year of the great depression.

Like I said, I knew when she stopped baking that things were going downhill fast.

And I was right. After the baking went, her church attendance flew out the window too. Consequently, so did mine. I suspected that she quit going to church partly because she was embarrassed for being fired, but mostly because she was just too depressed to get out of bed on Sunday mornings. After a couple months of poor attendance, Mama eventually quit going to church altogether. "Maggie, I just can't bring myself to get dressed and sit through one of those boring services. And, Shugah, right now, we can't really afford the church," she'd say. "And you know," she continued, "if I can't tithe, then I won't be able to use my gifts and teach Sunday school. If you don't cough up the money, they don't want you around! You are nothing but a dawggon, second class Christian if you can't pay your church dues."

I do declare! Back then, I really didn't care if we were second class citizens or not. Not having to attend church was a huge relief for me. At that point in time, I had no use for church at all. I was still mad at Reverend Stogging for making such a big deal out of those nice white mice and for firing Mama. That minister took away our spending money and my Mama's self-worth and I wouldn't forget it anytime soon. How could he have had such little compassion on a single woman who was trying her best to raise a child? I wouldn't have walked across the street to pour water on him if he was on fire.

So, for the next year, Mama kept to herself and I ended up being the parent—cooking meals and telling her when to get out of bed and put on her clothes so she could drive me to school. In her seclusion, Mama became well acquainted with mail order catalogs, including Spiegel, of course. She ordered everything from clothes to food, which eliminated the need for her to get out of the house. I was no spiritual giant, but even as a young church girl I could figure a few things out—even before I read my first ten pop psychology books that Mama had bought for me at a yard sale. My amateur analysis of the situation was that Mama was mad at God. Mad at the Almighty for not answering her prayers like she wanted Him to. Mad at the Holy One because He would not make my heathen father leave butt-ugly Ellen and come back to her. Yes, folks—that was it in a nut shell. God did not do what she wanted Him to do and she was pitching a hissy fit.

A week or so after I came to that conclusion, Mama got out of bed, pulled me aside and showed me a note she'd written and had hidden in a dresser drawer in her bedroom. It read:

Dearest Martin,

Night and day, I have been down on my knees praying to God that you would leave that butt-ugly Ellen woman and come back to me and Maggie. But no, my prayers did nothing but hit the ceiling. You are still with that home wrecker who is not worth the bullets it would take to blow her brains out. Since you've been gone, I feel that there is nothing left for me to live for and I might as well just go to be with our dear Lord and Savior, Jesus Christ. In the event that I get up my nerve and decide to take my life, send our Maggie to live with my rich sister, Justine, if you and your bow-legged bitch don't want her. That way, at least one of us can live in Mountain Brook.

Sincerely,
Careen

Did I fail to mention that Ellen was bow-legged?

When Mama tucked the note back in its place, I looked and saw her bottle of sleeping pills in the drawer. I pretended not to see and tried to hide how I felt about it. But the problem was that could never hide how I was feeling. My emotions were always written all over my face. When Mama saw my distress, she bent down and took my face in her hands with a firmness that frightened me. Then, looking me straight in the eyes, she told me, "If you dare tell anyone what you have just seen, I will give you a whipping you'll never forget." Mama had never hit me a lick in my whole life, but somehow I just knew that this threat was real and that my butt was a cupcake if I ever told.

This suicide threat, coupled with everything else got me to thinking that it might not be a bad idea if I started praying again. Finding out that Mama was thinking about killing herself had a way of jump-starting my prayer life. So, with much sincerity and a heart full of fear, I went to my bedroom, got down on my knees, and prayed in earnest.

Much to my surprise (oh, me of little faith), Mama woke up the next morning in a good mood, dressed, ate breakfast, and drove me to school. Then, when I came home from school, she was waiting for me in the kitchen with some freshly baked chocolate chip cookies that I loved so much. At six o'clock she fixed supper, sat down with me to eat, and by the grace of God, she said "grace" before our meal.

With Mama back on her feet again, I felt more secure than I remembered feeling in a long time. But, alongside the sense of stability was this horrible sadness waiting in the wings for me—waiting to descend on me like a big, bad, black vulture. Mama wasn't the only one who was hurting, but I couldn't talk to her about my pain because she had always been the type of woman who could barely handle her own.

So, instead of talking to Mama, I'd go to my room and lose myself in my music. I'd shut myself up in my room after Mama was asleep, play my Carole King music and cry until I was snot-nosed sick. If this soulful singer couldn't send me into a funk then nobody could. And, if the music wouldn't move me to tears, the tacky 70's décor would help me work up a good sob. Burnt orange shag carpet. Lime green knick-knacks. Metallic wall paper. I can feel a good cry coming on now.

Because Mama always depended on me to help bear her burdens, there was seldom room for me in our relationship. And to be honest with you, I was getting tired of it. Burned out and worn out. Mama's troubles were always in the spotlight. And mine—just a little bit of dust behind the stage curtains.

One of the few things that could help get my mind off of our all too serious lives was school. Unlike most kids my age, I liked school and I especially liked my English class because we read some of the best works in all of literature. *To Kill a Mockingbird* and *In Cold Blood* were my favorites. I did book reports on both because in my research I found out that Harper Lee and Truman Capote were friends back in Monroeville, Alabama.

At the end of each semester, I could not wait until the grades came out so that I could feel good about myself when I saw all the A's lined up neatly in a row on my orange report card. Being oriented toward performance, even my dispassionate, withholding, heathen father would have given me a kind word for this accomplishment. "Maggie," he'd say, lifting his nose out of a book momentarily, "making good grades and getting a good education is the most important thing in life. Your mother lives in a fantasy world thinking that Jesus is salvation, but I'm telling you that education and making a decent living is your salvation. So get yourself a good education and you won't need religion. Only weak people need religion—but don't tell your mama I said that."

His words rang in my head night after night as I was doing my homework. Weak people need religion? Weak people need religion?

Hmm.

But, didn't being a drunk and a fornicator make my father a weak person?

Chapter 10

Can you hear me?

Mama and her failed marriage. My heathen father and his emotional unavailability. If it seems to you like I was obsessed with my family problems the entire time I was growing up, then you have a firm grasp of the obvious.

But, somewhere amidst that obsession with others, I eventually found a way to attend to my pain. Secluding myself in my bedroom, I did what I'd been doing since about second grade—putting my thoughts and feelings down on paper. I shared my deepest thoughts with "Alice"—the journal that was tucked safely beneath my mattress. Every night before I fell asleep, I'd pour out my heart in that little 9 x 5 notebook telling "her" my deepest feelings. The fact that she didn't talk was the best part. Unlike Mama, Alice could do only one thing—listen. Sometimes I even wrote poems like my mother used to do when she was feeling down:

Wanting to run, wanting to hide,
Pockets of pain deep down inside of my heart
I need a healing love...
Old childhood fears, tug at my sleeve
Voices I hear, telling me not to believe
In Your healing love. . .

"Well, who wouldn't need healing after all that sick Irishman, Martin McBride, put us through," I said to myself while blaming God for my fate. "I needed a father and he was the best you could come up with, God? Why couldn't you give me a father like Sue's daddy? I, too, wanted a warm, fuzzy, teddy bear of a man who would bring presents and give me hugs and kisses. Why Martin, why him?"

Full of hurt and indignation, I was on the verge of pitching a fit. I could feel it coming on. Something uncontrollable was bubbling up to the surface of consciousness. Something powerful and unstoppable. Something was rising up inside of me, rising up like mighty torrents of water that had been held beneath the surface of the earth by dry and hardened ground. My insides were shaking. My heart was pounding almost like the time when I walked down the aisle and became a church girl.

So, with internal tension mounting to intolerable proportions, I took the pen that I was writing with and slung it down so hard that it bounced like a ball upon the pages of my journal. And with that action, it burst, leaking ink all over my poem and onto my sweaty palms. My fury steadily rising—I took that cheap thing in hand and hurled it up against the wall as hard as I possibly could. And this time—it splattered everywhere. On the walls. On my bedspread. On the floor.

Wanting to scream so badly that I thought my brain would explode to smithereens; I fought with myself to keep from doing it. If Mama were to have heard me screaming, she would have come into my room and then—God only knows what would have happened. No, I vowed not to lose complete control. So I bit down on my upper lip to contain myself and just sat there silently seething.

This church girl was livid while staring down at the stains on my hands from the tacky oversized fountain pen that my pitiful daddy had given to me for Christmas the year before he left. It was a quirky looking, red thing, about an inch around, with silver sparkles all over it.

While staring at the mess I noticed that my hands were shaking. Trying to steady them, I turned my palms upward and tried to rub the ink from my skin. But you and I both know that it was futile. Removing the stains from my hands would have been much easier, however, than removing the dark and dangerous stains of rejection and loneliness from my heart.

In that moment, I knew that something strange was happening to me. I began to feel dizzy, split-off, weightless and very much alike being asleep or in a dream. It felt as though my body and soul were separated. I experienced a floating sensation like being out at sea and lost on the waves.

So, mindlessly, in a delirious disassociation, I drifted across the room, bent down and gently picked up the broken pen. Seeing that the silver prong on the side was still attached—but now all sharp and catawampus, it occurred to me, that—well . . . the pen was special. The pen would help me silence my fears. The pen would help make the pain go away if just for a moment. The pen would help to put the hurt on the outside so that the pain on the inside of me could take a rest.

And so, I decided to do the forbidden.

I held the pen lovingly, tenderly, and carefully in my hand. I positioned the silver prong on the tiny vein above my pulse. My heart was beating wildly, but strangely, I did not feel alive.

Ba-bump, ba-bump, ba-bump went the sound of my heart pounding in my head.

I hadn't been alive, not really, since I was very young and still held hope that my father would love me.

Ba-bump, ba-bump, ba-bump.

And so, I crossed the line between sanity and insanity.

It was pure comfort and ecstasy—feeling that jagged, but sharp prong carve a magnificent red track into my lily-white wrist. I slashed deliberately and slowly as if to prolong the agony and feel it deeply. Delicious, soothing pain washed over me. And the best part—the very best part was afterwards, when the deed was complete. For the first time in my life, I felt all of the pain… leave. It was such a sweet, sinful release.

Then, when my heart had settled from its unruly panic, and while I was basking in the afterglow of the painful pleasure, an eerie stillness fell softly upon my anxious soul. But after I felt that false sense of peace, I felt something worse: overwhelming, unbearable guilt. And I knew at that moment from the depths of my soul that I would not use that pen, ever again. For in that one act of self-injury, I discovered an evil comfort meant only for those who don't know what else to do with their feelings.

But, just in case you are self-righteous, and just in case you are sitting there judging me and thinking I'm twisted and crazy, I'll tell you something: cutters don't really want to hurt themselves. They just want the pain in their hearts to go away. And more than wanting to be free of emotional pain, more than anything else in the world—they want you to know that they have a voice.

They want to be heard.

Once, when I told someone about my bout with self-harm, the person told me that I had no business reacting to the hurts of my childhood in this manner because I was not physically beaten or sexually abused. The person told me that cutting myself because of the pain of my past was overblown, exaggerated and dramatized.

And if you are thinking this way too, this church girl wants to set the record straight.

I want to tell you once and for all that to be shunned and ignored by your father on a daily basis the entire time you are growing up was nothing more than chronic abuse. I want to tell you that to have lived in the house with your parent who did not even know what grade of school you were in, what school you attended or how old you were was maddening. I want to tell you that to have been taught that your feelings about being rejected and unloved were bad and wrong was nothing less than torture.

I remembered that after I comforted my sickened self, I went into the bathroom and ran water over my wild and wonderful wound. Curiously, I watched my own fresh blood trickle slowly down the sink as I washed my hands. The sight of it was surreal. It was as if I were watching someone else bleeding. Not me. Not this cynical church girl.

Cutting my wrist felt so right, but at the same time—everything in me knew that it was wrong. I had been a very, very bad girl. A dirty, dirty sinner. "Oh what should I do?" I murmured to myself on that day. "Tell Mama? Call the prayer chain?"

No. No. No. I couldn't tell anyone. "No one would understand," I thought. And so, deciding not to speak of this incident to a living soul, I did come to my senses and did the responsible, mature thing. I bandaged my wrist, concealed my affliction and tried my best to sleep.

Would it be a surprise if I told you that I had a horrible nightmare?

In the nightmare, Mama and I were in a red convertible driving along a very narrow strip of road that went straight out into a vast ocean. There were no guardrails on the road. There was nothing to protect us from falling into the water. Any move to the right or to the left could send us plummeting to our deaths. To make matters worse, there was a huge statue up ahead (that consisted of three separate parts) as tall as the tallest skyscraper. The statue was a cold, dispassionate-looking metal sculpture of God the Father, God the Son and God the Holy Spirit. Each of the sculpture parts was holding a massive sword in his hand and twirling it at the same time. While looking upon this monstrosity, it came to me; this is a test. Somehow, Mama and I were required to calculate the exact moment when we could drive between those twirling swords and escape being cut to pieces or impaled by the instruments of torture. One wrong calculation, one wrong move, and God in three persons would cut us to pieces. We got one chance to save ourselves and we had to do it perfectly. One chance. That was all. Only one!

I awoke suddenly in a panic. Dripping with sweat. Heart racing. I was certain that I knew the meaning of the dream. The meaning was that He—God, that is, demanded perfection from us. Exactness. Precision. Flawlessness. That pompous preacher of my childhood must have been right; God was an angry man just like my father. How could I doubt it now, since the dream had come to me and proven that this was so? After coming to that sick conclusion, I was distraught, I was devastated. "I will never be able to live up to God's demands," I thought. "I will never be able to please Him. If I can't be a perfect church girl, I might as well just quit trying."

Dear reader, in all honestly, in addition to my fear, I was reluctant to surrender my life to God because I was sure that if I did, He would surely make me do something that would be totally scary and unappealing to me—like sending me to work in the darkest jungle of Africa with the pygmies, or that He would exercise His almighty power to strike my body with a miserable illness that would leave me paralyzed. These tormenting thoughts ran through my mind whenever I thought about yielding my life to God.

In my distress, in my absolute terror over dealing with this wretchedness, I went to my guidance counselor at school and told her about the dream. I had hoped she would offer some spiritual insight or consolation. But, when I finished talking, she looked at me as if I needed to be committed to a mental institution and said, "You have a very active imagination. Did you happen to eat pizza last night?" Then, she smiled as if I were profoundly silly and changed the subject. She told me that believing in God was nonsense, and then she said, "Tell me about your home life, Maggie."

While waiting for my answer, she cocked her head to one side and drummed her fingernails on the table...click...click...click...and so I began telling stories of my home life just to stop that irritating noise. I shared a few stories about living with Careen and Martin—the good, the bad and the ugly. And when the counselor wasn't yawning, she nodded her head and smiled. When half an hour had passed, she sighed and said something that was incredibly common in the seventies, "You know, Maggie, I think you have low self-esteem."

Her diagnosis was low self-esteem. Low self-esteem! Are you surprised?

In the seventies, low self-esteem was the explanation for everything. Serial killers had low self-esteem. Angry dogs had low self-esteem. Colicky babies had low self-esteem. Depressed mothers had low self-esteem.

So Mrs. Pettyjohn had me work on my low self-esteem. She gave me little booklets on self-respect to read and had me write out on paper twenty things I liked about myself. Then, I had to fill out a series of worksheets that asked astute questions: "What is your happy place? What color makes you feel the most alive? What are three things that you can do for yourself to make you feel loved?"

Even after listing and discussing this list of brilliant questions, I still had low self-esteem plus the hidden issues of anger, bitterness, and unforgiveness in my heart. As important and earth-shattering as these questions and answers were they didn't fix my problem. With her pop psychology help, I ended up being angrier, bitterer and more unforgiving than ever before. At Mama. At Father. At Ellen. And at the person who could have helped me the most—God. Any healing that could have happened in this area was hijacked by the distraction of focusing on my lack of self-esteem.

Low self-esteem? Wrong diagnosis. That was just the tip of the iceberg. If she had been listening carefully, she would have known that the problem was much, much deeper. It wasn't low self-esteem, it was self-righteousness and bitterness that was stuck to me like white on rice.

Can you hear me?

CHAPTER 11

TONGUE SANDWICHES

MAMA NEVER FOUND OUT ABOUT the cutting or about Mrs. Pettyjohn. And, give or take a couple of months (after Mama came out of her depression), she got back into the church scene, but in a different way. It was as if she was starting all over with her faith, venturing out to find her own identity as a woman in the Christian community. And, of course, like a good little church girl's church girl, I went with her.

Over the course of a year, we visited all kinds of churches—More Southern Baptist churches, Pentecostal, Charismatic, Episcopalian, Church of Christ and oodles of others. But, because we were somewhat rough around the edges with our practice of religion, it was hard to find a church where we felt like we fit in.

In the Southern Baptist church, we learned more about evangelism, and were reminded that women could not preach— even if God called them to do it. In the Pentecostal church, we were taught how to speak in tongues and go without makeup. In the charismatic church, we learned undue reverence for ministers and how to "name it and claim it." In the Episcopal Church, we learned about The Book of Common Prayer, and when to stand, when to kneel, when to sit and (thank God) when to quit. When we attended the Church of Christ, they told us that God hated instrumental music in church, which was a very low blow to us because, as you know, Mama played the piano.

After months of going from church to church, we were so religiously screwed up we probably needed an exorcist! But, in spite of this foolishness, we were determined to press on. During each religious encounter, we jumped eagerly into the church culture and tried to make their doctrinal quirks and rules our own.

In each fellowship we attended, Mama scanned the pews for female role models whom she could imitate; ones that looked like they had it all together. But no women stepped up to the plate to mentor us until we visited a lively group called Woman Fire and . . . voila!—dozens of women appeared out of nowhere who were ready and willing to take us under their wings and mould us into the perfect church girls!

Every woman we met wanted to make us her latest project in hopes that we could be conformed to the church's cultural norms. Halleluiah. Some women sought to change the way we dressed, some women scrutinized what style and type of Bible holder we were carrying, and some women evaluated the type of sermons we listened to when we were not at church. Others took a more interior approach to their scrutiny—rummaging through our lives to hunt for hidden sins that may have been keeping us from God's favor. A small percentage of women took on the role of critical parent—condemning our personalities and the way we expressed our spirituality.

On any given day, you could hear the women engaging in dialogue like this:

> *Mama: Could you tell me where I can find the ladies' rest room?*
>
> *Righteous Rita: Well, Honey, it's down the hall to the right, but you know that Jesus said, "Come to me and I will give you rest." If you were closer to God, the Holy Spirit would have revealed the exact location to you and you would not have needed to ask someone for directions. The only reason that Christians can't hear His voice is because they don't spend enough time in prayer and fellowship with God. About how much time do you spend alone with God in prayer?*
>
> *Mama: Well, about an hour...*
>
> *Righteous Rita: See, there's your dad-gum problem. You need*

to pray more. Much, much more. God told me to tell you that this was your blessed moment. He told me to tell you that He put me in your path so that I can help you organize your schedule to fit more time for prayer into your day. And when you do, then God will speak to you and give you guidance. Then you will not be so flustered that you'll have to ask someone for directions to get to a rest room.

Well, well, well. By the time Righteous Rita had finished her sanctimonious lecture; Mama had peed in her pants and had a whole other set of shame issues to deal with.

Bless Mama's poor unsuspecting heart. In the naiveté of her new spirituality coupled with her desperate need for approval, she had happened upon a brood of overly confident and controlling church girls who intended to make her over in their own image.

As if the bossy church girls weren't bad enough, there was something that bothered me even more.

But first, a little background information.

There exists such a thing in some churches that I call a "tongue sandwich." Now, I'm not talking about what Mama used to feed me when I was little—a slice of cow tongue between two slices of white bread with tomatoes, lettuce and mayonnaise. What I'm talking about is more serious than that. I'm talking about the spiritually abusive practice of trapping a poor unsuspecting victim like a piece of meat between two slices of bread while coercing a person into speaking in tongues.

Picture this: Mama and I were at a Thursday night meeting of Woman Fire. The teaching was over, the fat lady had sung and Roz (the woman in charge) was getting ready to speak. "Listen up," she said to the women who came to the meeting. "We have a little saying in our beloved group:

> *We speak in tongues.*
> *We all do.*
> *And if you want to fit in here,*
> *All y'all's will, too."*

After reciting the silly little poem, Roz bantered, "So, don't be shy or I'll have to come and get your sanctified butts out of your seat and take you down front. Don't make me do it. Any volunteers? Come on now. Don't be shy for Jesus."

After a long pause, a couple of timid gals raised their hands. But before they could get them all the way up in the air, Roz went over to where they were sitting, jerked them up out of their seats and dragged them down front. Then, as if rehearsed and on cue, her prayer team rushed over to the prospective tongue-talkers and gathered around those women like a brood of vultures ready to close in on their prey.

Merciless, they targeted Hannah, volunteer number one. They prayed loudly for her and wham, bam, thank you mam—Hannah was a fast, tongue-talkin' machine—"Hannah-bo-banna-banana-nana-fo-fanna-fee-fie-mo-manna-hannah!"

And then—there came person number two, Dorothy.

Uh-oh, the women prayed for her to receive tongues but absolutely nothing came out of her mouth. Nothing.

The women on the prayer team looked suspiciously at each other as if they had failed. Discouraged, but still determined to get Dot to flip her lips—they prayed again. "Oh, Lo-red. Send down the tongues!"

Still nothing.

Seeing that the woman was standing there with her mouth hanging open—two eager prayer warriors moved in closer and flanked her like she was a piece of meat between two slices of bread.

Behold—the tongue sandwich!

Decisively, they motioned for more fiery women to make a circle around her so that she could not escape the next part of the abuse. . .

> *Righteous Rita: Come on girl, you can do it! The Word says that they spake as the spirit gave them utterance, so speak, Dot, speak!*
>
> *Holy Helen: Dot, you're not speaking in tongues, what is wrong with you? Is there sin in your life? Unbelief? Gum in your mouth? Oh wait, Dot, let me help you. Just bark out something like chitty-chitty-bang-bang to get you started.*
>
> *Sanctified Sue: If that doesn't work, say do-wah-diddy-diddy-dum-diddy-do. What, Dot? You're still not tongue-ing?*

Not getting the response they wanted, the women were getting *really* frustrated, so one of the older toxic church girls resorted to the following. . .

> *Catty Cassie: Here, Dot. Simmer down now and listen to me: She-came-in-on-a-Honda-come-tie-my-bow-tie.*

As she said this, she cupped her hand around the person's ear and spoke really slooooowly.

But much to their dismay, even after their best attempts at the tongues training session, Dot still didn't speak. She just stood there looking sad and traumatized. Occasionally she would glance at her captors through big brown, pleading eyes.

See Dot run!

After this travesty, I'm sure Dot felt lower than a weenie dog with mange. She'd been shamed and accused of having sin in her life because she couldn't speak on command. Poor Dottie! She was the latest victim of the tongue sandwich. And just as I would have done after coming to my senses, Dot bolted out of the door never to be seen at Woman Fire again.

Run, Dot, run.

Without a doubt, Mama and I had a lot of strange experiences while she was trying to define herself in the Christian Community. And this one was at the top of the list. After this weird experience with the toxic church girls and the tongue sandwich, I was sure that Mama would settle for a nice, sedate, denominational church. But once again, I was wrong. As soon as she recovered from Woman Fire, she decided to jump from the frying pan into the fire. She said she was ready to try another charismatic church.

Isn't that just precious?

Chapter 12

Addicted to Prayer Lines

Well, of course, Mama wanted to try another charismatic church since her inner saint was outgoing, expressive and dramatic. The whole charismatic movement in the eighties was full of these personality types. How else could they have those lively, entertaining services?

Only five miles away from where we were living at the time, Mama decided that we'd try a new fellowship called The Church of Great Feelings. Well, having such a captivating name, I could understand why she'd want to try it at least once. Even a non-believer might have visited out of sheer curiosity.

And curious it was. After being there about three weeks, Mama and I decided that the church *definitely* lived up to its name. Every service was lively, action-packed and *very* emotional. If someone wasn't clapping, dancing, shouting or falling out on the floor then the Pastor told us that it wasn't a good service and that he wasn't pleased.

So, in an effort to please the pastor, most of the congregation made it a point to be as flamboyantly expressive as possible during worship. Sometimes it looked as if each member of the congregation was trying to outdo the other members with their dramatic display of emotions, all of this as a means of winning the pastor's approval.

And no one tried harder than a perky young woman in the congregation named Clementine.

Clementine was one of those "prodigal converts." Having been a hellion in college, upon graduation she gave her life to God, cut down on drinking and began to search for a church home. While driving down the road one Sunday morning, Clementine told me that she happened to see the marquee in our church yard that read, "Get Drunk on New Wine at The Church of Great Feelings" and (in her own words), "my car nearly drove itself right into the parking lot." She told us that a little voice told her that The Church of Great Feelings was "the place she ought to be so she swerved into our parking lot and met the Reverend Reed." Hearing that line, made me sad to think that she had just ruined the theme song to "The Beverly Hillbillies!"

So very happy to have yet another member of The Church of Great Feelings, the pastor welcomed her with open arms and, in no time flat, she swore off alcohol altogether and ended up medicating her undesirable feelings of insecurity with another drug of choice.

As soon as she got off tequila and moonshine, she became. . .

Addicted to prayer lines.

You heard me right. Clementine became a prayer line addict—a person overcome by the compulsion to be prayed over in a prayer line. It was the cunning, baffling and powerful force that started out giving her positive results but ended up being the idol that drove her to destruction. Or that is what the AA people would have told her.

Around two-thirty one Sunday, just before the altar call, Clementine (who didn't waste any time making herself known) apparently felt the Spirit during the ministry time and starting dancing around the church doing what looked like a cross between a rooster strutting and some aberrant form of disco.

When I saw her drawing attention to herself with her odd gyrations, and I, not being able to contain myself, gasped aloud--Oooahhhhh! And when I did, I must have gotten her attention, because she boogied on over to where Mama and I were sitting, took me by the hand and dragged me down to the altar. And then, in the most heartfelt way, she said, "Now, honey, I know that you didn't mean no harm but you need to repent for interrupting my super-spiritual moment."

"I didn't mean to interrupt your super-spiritual moment," I said. "It's just that I've never seen anyone do anything like that in church before. It is very attention getting. Very."

"Really? You mean I stood out among the others?" she said, as her eyes flickered with narcissistic delight.

"Yes, you did. Really!" I answered. "You *really* did."

Well, when I saw how serious she was about her super-spiritual moment, I began to doubt my gut feeling about her being a "show out." Maybe she was sincere and I was just too skeptical and not super-spiritual.

Well, after she convinced me of the sincerity of her super-spiritual moment, I felt awful and found myself apologizing profusely for doubting her intentions. After our hour-long stay at the altar, listening to her tell me all about herself, I found myself actually liking the strange creature who wanted to be my new friend.

So, in a very short time, nineteen-year-old Clementine had worked her way into my life and was acting like a big super-spiritual sister. Surprisingly, instead of being wary of this unusual girl, Mama liked her too, and didn't mind letting her into our well-guarded lives.

Week after week, there we were, all three of us, sitting on the front pew at The Church of Great Feelings, eager to partake in everything the charismatic congregation had to offer. For a season, we couldn't have been happier if we had died and gone to Heaven. It seemed like we were the church girls with everything—our touchy-feely church, our charismatic preacher, our bumper stickers with the fish on them and a mouth full of holy babble. Kumbaya. Kumbay'all. Kumba-all-y'all. A-men.

But even with all of this paraphernalia and holy babble, there was a part of me that knew something was missing. I had it all going on, on the outside, but still felt empty on the inside. In my heart of hearts, I was still holding God at arm's length because of the fear that had entered me at age nine in that little Baptist church so long ago that had never gone away.

Oh, it was easy to do the outward religious acts. I could sing and clap and pray with the best of them, and still not connect with God. And the pitiful thing was that nobody (including the preacher) knew the difference. I found out quickly that if you make an outward show of religiosity, you could make people believe that you are a committed Christian. Even more so if you are person like Clementine who made sure she was seen every Sunday up front in a prayer line.

Nope, Clementine was not content unless she could be in the limelight. So serious and out of control was her obsession, that one week, when the preacher at the Wednesday night service made the altar call and told people to come and get in the prayer line, Clementine fell all over me trying to bolt out of the pew to get up front. Yes, brothers and sisters, before I could even rub the pain out of my sore shin she grabbed me by the hand and said, "Let's go, Sister. I'm gonna get my fix. It's prayer time!"

And so, away we went.

While standing in the line awaiting my turn, my newfound friend forgot all about her Southern raising and became as rude as a New York Yankee. Instead of waiting her turn like a decent person, she greedily pushed ahead of everyone else in the prayer line so that she could be first. Seeing that she was so eager, the preacher pulled out a vial of anointing oil out of his pocket and said, "You, yes you, my darlin' Clementine, get over here."

"Oh my," I thought to myself, "I've seen this on Christian TV, but I've never seen it in real life. The preacher is actually going to lay hands on her and anoint her with oil just like it said in the Bible!"

And so, he prayed for her and then slapped her on top of the head so hard that I imagined she saw stars. And when he did, something strange happened: The girl fell slap out on the floor. Slain in the Spirit, they called it. She looked dead as a doornail. Maybe deader. And when she fell, everyone around me became wide-eyed and began to mutter things like, "I told you that she was a very spiritual girl! She must pray, fast and sleep on a bed of nails for that to happen to her!"

Well, after seeing Clementine all sprawled out on the church floor with a blanket thrown over her bare legs (a blanket that coordinated beautifully with the color of the church carpet) I became jealous of her. After all, Clementine was looking so very spiritual that I decided to have that minister pray for me so that I could make a spiritual impression in front of all those people too. I wanted the same deal. The prayer. The slap. The works. If she could fall, then I could fall, too.

And so, I did. Ka-plunk!

And this, dear friends, concluded my first experience with the prayer line.

But, just like Clementine, after that one awesome experience, I had a strong desire to repeat the incident as soon as possible. I really liked the feelings and the special attention, so I reasoned with myself, "If a little public prayer is good then more is better." So, I started coming to The Church of Great Feelings every Wednesday night to ask for prayer.

Every time the preacher extended the invitation, I found myself zipping off to get in a prayer line quicker than a coon dog after a squirrel. If I didn't have a serious prayer concern, I would request prayer for the trivial—a pimple, a hangnail, or bad breath. Nothing mattered, just as long as I could bask in those heavenly feelings and get that attention.

Just like Clementine, I quickly went from experimental use to being a regular "prayerliner." Soon, yes, very soon, Clementine and I became discontented with those experiences and, wouldn't you know it, we found another church where they held prayer line meetings three times a week.

Our first time visiting this "hyper-prayer line" church, the pastor asked for the congregation to form a line so that he could lay hands on people, anoint them with oil and prophesy. Prophesy? Sounded good to Clementine and me. And with this spiritual combination of prayer-plus-oil-plus-prophecy, that's all it took, Clementine was hooked. And so was I. At this new church, we could get prayed for and have hands laid on us three times a week whether we needed it or not! And with the additional perk of prophecy, we could cut back on our own private devotional times with God—who needed them when someone could hear from God for us!

After this, our addiction progressed rapidly. Before long we were not content with the three times per week "fixes." It just wasn't enough to satisfy us. We were becoming very dependent upon the feelings we'd get when we were ministered to, and so we began to tell ourselves that unless we could actually feel those goose bumps and get a high sensation when we were being prayed for, we were not spiritual and God was not affirming us. Can you believe that?

Before long our whole life centered on our addiction. Once, when we were prayer seeking, we sneaked inside an Episcopal Church and got into their line. All of a sudden, we noticed that we were the only ones who were not wearing a robe. It was at that moment that the bishop tapped us on the head with his staff and sternly informed us that we were in a procession, not a prayer line, and we could kindly sit our attention-seeking selves down! We were utterly humiliated to say the least, but even *this* event did not stop us from engaging in the addictive behavior.

After months of going from church to church, prayer group to prayer group, home group to home group meeting—just anywhere we thought we could be prayed for, we realized that because of all of the hands that had been laid on top of our heads our necks were beginning to hurt so badly that we could not sleep! As the pain increased, our denial began to break and finally, we had to face the fact that we had been wounded as a result of all of the vigorous, excitable praying.

Some ministers who put their hands on us were respectful and sensitive, but others were like brute, mad men, screaming and yelling when they prayed for us as if God were deaf and dumb. These aggressive types didn't seem to realize how much force they were using, leaving us with a good case of whiplash. They screamed, "Be healed!" at the top of their lungs and palmed our heads like a basketball! Slam dunk—it hurt like hell. In an effort to minimize the pain, we started using the courtesy fall.

What in God's creation is that, you may be thinking . . .

Well, the courtesy fall is when you go ahead and voluntarily fall whenever a forcible minister pushes on your head. You willingly fall because you're concerned about the possibility of getting your neck broken or receiving other physical injuries if you don't fall quickly. So, Clementine and I did our first courtesy fall in order to save our necks from being broken and, secondarily, to trick the minister into thinking that he had done his job and was indeed a *super-anointed* and *very powerful* individual.

This is when I hit rock bottom.

After about six months of this nonsense, when Mama got tired of hearing me complain about my aching neck, she insisted that I stop getting prayed on. Resisting her command, I insisted that I could control my use of charismatic prayer, if I really wanted to control it.

"Mama, I can quit prayer-lining anytime I want to quit. I swear I can. Just say the word and I'll quit doing lines."

But Mama didn't believe me anymore since she saw me frequently rubbing my neck and hitting the aspirin bottle when I got home. Being concerned that her only child may have sustained an injury, she made me an appointment with Dr. Thompson—a chiropractor.

Secretly hoping that the doc would help me get out of pain, I eagerly cooperated with him while he took a series of x-rays. When the x-ray films were developed, he came back into the exam room and started asking questions. When he asked if I had ever had a bad fall, and pointed to the injured disc on the x-ray, I just about fainted. There it was in black and white—a picture of my poor neck. That temptress, Clementine, had seduced me with her addiction and I ended up with my own addiction. Isn't that just like the Devil?

So I "fessed up" as Aunt Justine used to say. I swallowed my pride and "fessed up." I broke down and told him about the prayer lines and the excitable preachers, and Clementine and the slam dunks with my noggin and—the lifesaving courtesy fall. When I was finished with my stories, I will never forget the look on that doctor's face. He looked at me as if I had three heads! And if looks could kill, he flashed a mean one in my Mama's direction.

"In my professional opinion," he began, "that Charismatic Clementine person with whom you are allowing your daughter to associate is brainwashing your child. And you. . . dear woman, are abusing her by encouraging her to participate in. . . how shall I put this? A charismatic cult. Because of this nonsense, your child is going to be on muscle relaxers for the next few months until she gets better. And, Mrs. McBride, if you don't do something to prevent this girl from engaging in these strange and dangerous practices, I am going to call social services and report you for child abuse. It's your choice. Are you going to end this nonsense, or risk losing your child? I want your answer right now or I *will* pick up the phone and make that call!"

"No, you don't have to do that," she said nervously. "Consider her prayer-lining days over even as we speak. Never again. I promise. Do you hear me, Maggie, no more lines."

Holy cow, that man scared the pee out of Mama. After hearing his chastisement, she was so embarrassed and afraid of losing me that she forbade me from ever calling or seeing Clementine again. "I should have known that you'd get in trouble by hanging out with that Holy Roller," she said. "I forbid you to ever see that girl again!"

"Mama," I replied, "You encouraged it, too!"

"Do as I say and cut it off with that girl or you will be in your room until Hell freezes over," Mama snapped.

As we all know, you don't argue with a Southern mama when she is protecting her only chick. Furthermore, I knew that Hell wasn't going to freeze over in my lifetime, so I had no choice but to obey. And the only way that I could get Clementine out of my life for good was to leave The Church of Great Feelings.

So, in my best interest, I said goodbye to charismania, goodbye to that *dreadful, sorry* Clementine, and goodbye to all the neck injuries I got in the prayer lines. Being true to our word at the doctor's office, Mama and I said goodbye to The Church of Great Feelings because the great feelings it promised just turned into great pain.

Bye, y'all.

And so, once again, this mother and daughter team was churchless. Once again we had become spiritual vagabonds, wandering pilgrims, and wayfaring strangers who were seeking that perfect place of belonging in the religious world.

Would we ever find what we were looking for?

CHAPTER 13

DÉJÀ MOO: THE SENSE THAT YOU HAVE EXPERIENCED THIS BULL BEFORE.

ONE DAY, WHEN MAMA AND I were tired of driving here, there and everywhere, trying to find a church home, we stayed at home on a Sunday afternoon to watch *Gone with the Wind* for probably the hundredth time. Well, right when Rhett Butler was telling Miss Scarlett that he doesn't "give a damn," the visitor from Hell—a sneaky minion of Mr. Satan showed up on our doorstep.

I remember it as if it were yesterday.

The doorbell rang. Mama answered it. There that devil stood. Six foot five, big wavy hair and intense brown eyes with a mesmerizing quality that made the hairs on the back on my neck stand up.

"Hello," he said as he shoved a church brochure into my Mama's opened hand and started talking faster than an auctioneer on speed. "My name is Jimmy Ray Walker. I pastor the church around the corner and I'd like to invite you our Wednesday night suppers. You'll eat some of the best Southern cookin' you've ever tasted in your life: fried chicken, green beans, mashed potatoes, cornbread and some of that good ol' banana pudding for dessert. And ... there's a great group for young people that your girl here, would like. I'm sorry, I don't mean to be rude...I don't know your name."

"Careen," Mama replied.

"Careen," he crooned. "Oh my, sister-saint, that's a real purdy name and what is your purdy girl's name?"

"Maggie."

"Maggie? Well butter my biscuit; she's as cute as a speckled pup hooked to a red wagon! I just know that you and your little Magpie would fit right in at The Flow."

"The Flow? That sounds interesting," Mama said, cocking an eyebrow.

"Yes sister-saint, the Lord came to me in a dream and told me exactly what to call it."

"Came to you in a dream? Did He really, now?" Mama said.

"Yes, he did sister-saint. The Lord came to me in a dream and told me exactly what to call it. It was the same night that the Lord (in the form of a bright psychedelic light) visited me in my bathroom while I was fixin' my hair and told me that He had a plan and purpose for my life and that I'd better get with the program and go with the flow! You see sister-saint; I was acting worse than a hell-bent heathen before I came to the Lord. I was drinking, smoking, and womanizing. I was on the highway to Hell without a spare tire. But then, that rotten, dreadful night when the Spirit came to me, I took a good look at the ruggedly handsome man in the mirror (with the tattoo of my Pitt Bull, Shredder, on my arm) and I knew for sure that this stud was going straight to Hell if I did not change my evil ways. Yep, after that encounter with the "Man Upstairs," I threw away the bottles, snuffed out the cigarettes, ditched the whores and got hooked on God. I got in the flow, sister-saint! In the flow!"

"You don't say," I said sarcastically. "Oh brother," I thought to myself. Magpie? Sister-saint? Where did this man come from? Oh, yes. I know. Could it be Podunk City, Alabama? He might have thought he was pretty smart, but with his manner of expression, I thought that he was dumber than road kill.

"I do say little sister!" he said and continued with his crazy-talk. "And then the Lord spoke to me again like He did with Moses at that burning bush and said, "Jimmy Ray," and I said, "Speak, Lord, for your servant listens," and the Lord continued, "As a reward I'm going to give you one power-packed church. It's not going to be your typical church. No-sir-ree-bob-tail. It's going to be a church that will be flowing and going, going and flowing!"

Well, after that hunky-dory sales pitch, I thought that Mama would have sent him packing, but nopity-nope-nope-nope, the silly woman invited him in for coffee and cobbler.

"Oh, my, my, my, ain't this the most delicious dessert in Dixie?" Jimmy Ray exclaimed as he finished sucking down the last few scrumptious blueberries. Before Mama could get the dirty bowl into the kitchen sink, Jimmy Ray was flirting with her like he had never even heard the God who had previously spoken to him with a Southern accent and said "No-sir-ree-bob-tail" –if you believe that crap.

He was a real flirt, that counterfeit preacher man. He complimented Mama's hair, her dress, the shape of her lips. And after he was through *lusting* after her, the man turned to me and started more nonsense—"Oh, what a purdy little girl you have; I bet she's a real heartbreaker with that fiery red hair! She's almost as beautiful as that life-size picture you have of Scarlett O'Hara hanging over your couch."

Yes. Mama still had the picture.

I glared at him mercilessly. Didn't like him from the get-go, no-sir-ree-bob-tail, I didn't!

"Where did she get those auburn locks?" he said. "I'll bet her daddy had red hair, didn't he?"

"Yes, he did." Mama said flippantly.

"How dare he mention my daddy," I thought.

When that preacher saw the angry look on my face because of that comment, he just upped the flattery. After three or four more admirations directed at Mama, he gazed around our house like a salesman looking for a point of contact so that he could close a deal. Steely eyes scanning the room, he finally spied the piano and coaxed Mama to play for him.

"Well, lookie here...which one of you lovely ladies plays the piano?"

Lookie? Really? Lookie? This self-proclaimed preacher man was sitting in our living room using words like "lookie." I could have puked. That man was a mixture of good ol' boy, redneck, hillbilly, and po' white trash, bless his heart. He was countrified as cornflakes. While I was criticizing his vocabulary in the privacy of my mind, Mama pulled out the sheet music to "His Eye is on the Sparrow" and flawlessly played the beautiful tune as if she were not being watched by those dark demonized eyes.

Well folks, to make a long sob story short, that one song tuned into a concert, and that concert turned into a three-hour conversation, and that conversation turned into a first date, and the first date turned into a second date, and a second date turned into a third date, and then, with God as my witness, in less than a year they were married.

Trust me: I was heartbroken.

And, in less than two years—my mother would be heartbroken, too.

And so, in no time flat this church girl had a new preacher and a new stepfather—and not just any ordinary stepfather, a stepfather with a PH.D. Not an academic degree like my real father, but…a Pentecostal Hair-Do.

When I think about living with Jimmy Ray, I see him standing in front of the bathroom mirror fixing his mullet with Alberto VO5 hairdressing, Dippity-Do hair gel and White Rain hair spray. The obsession with his hair often caused me to be late for school. He shampooed. He blow-dried. He applied some goopy drugstore products on it. And when he finished primping, he strutted out of the bathroom looking like a wild-eyed, redneck TV evangelist.

Although the mullet-man seemed quite pleased with his slick self, I wasn't impressed. I had to endure being cooped up in a car with the stink of cheap hair products and his second-hand religion all the way to school. While I choked on smelly hair fumes, Jimmy Ray would pop in a teaching tape by the renowned evangelist, Samuel Hargis Ignites Theford, memorize it word-for-word and then pass it off as his own creation the following Sunday when he preached at church. I suppose he thought that I was too dumb to notice that he was breaking the seventh commandment—"Thou shalt not steal" and that I was also too dumb to notice that the initial letters of the evangelist's name, Samuel Hargis Ignites Theford, spelled out the word "SHIT."

I was onto Jimmy Ray. I had to be. Who else was going to protect my Mama?

He was *scary*.

Having seen oodles of Christian praise-a-thons with Mama, I was certain that at any moment he would be making a pitch for me to give him my lunch money as an offering to support his ministry. But, so help me God, I was not going to give that quirky man a cent. My powers of discernment told me that Jimmy Ray Walker wasn't anything but a wolf in sheep's clothing. Unfortunately, that's something Mama would have to figure out in her own time.

The fact that I did not love him did not seem to bother him one whit. What irritated him to death was the fact that I neither respected nor admired him. "I don't care if you love me or not," he'd yell, "but you are going to respect me!" And of course, there was not a snowball's chance in Hell that I'd respect him because I could not respect a hypocrite.

He talked about God constantly—God told me this…God told me that…blah, blah, blah, but wouldn't give Mother or me the time of day—even when he was driving me to school. He was too engrossed in his Christian teaching tapes or the latest in Southern gospel music to get out of his world and into mine.

God may not have given me the gift of preaching, but He did give me the gift of discernment to know when someone is bullshitting me. Jimmy Ray bullshitted all of us on a regular basis and just like my father who convinced my mother that his professorship was so important and time-consuming that he had no time for a wife and child, Jimmy Ray's evangelical bent was at the center of his attention.

Jimmy Ray's religious addiction was just as powerful as my father's chemical addiction. I could tell that he got his ego boost from his position as a pastor—an ego also inflated by the adoring women who looked up to him at church. He quit womanizing? Right. He merely cloaked his interest in women under the guise of spiritual concern and mentorship. The man had a dad-gum harem.

These poor, pathetic, abused and needy women were in love with him, fighting among themselves for a favored position. The women used various tactics to gain his favor: they brought him gifts; they gave exorbitant offerings; they volunteered to work at the church; they brought food by our house. It was the most pitiful thing I had ever witnessed—these wretched women wasting their lives on a married man who was using them to boost his ego. But, more pathetic than that was the sorry fact that Jimmy Ray had my mother convinced that this was pastoring as usual. He reminded me of my heathen father who was married to Mama while fornicating with Ellen.

There was one big difference though—Jesus-loving Jimmy Ray wasn't as smart as my father. I often thought it funny how Mama could fall in love and marry a cold, detached intellectual and then do a 180-degree turnabout and get hitched to a lively, Pentecostal redneck.

But, in the final analysis, there was not much difference between the two men. My father was unavailable to us because of his selfishness, books and girlfriend. Jimmy Ray was unavailable to us because of his selfishness, religion and his holy harem.

Mama had done it again. Married the same man, but in a different package.

Sad, but true. Déjà Moo.

I had experienced that bull before.

Chapter 14

Heebie Jeebies.
Translation: A Full Body Shiver

"Heebie Jeebies" is a good old Southern saying that means "full body shiver." This is exactly what I felt each time I thought about my stepfather, Jimmy Ray Walker. Even with his funky hair and his unholy harem (two glaring red flags that Mama should have noticed before she married the po-dunk fella), Jimmy Ray had managed to deceive my poor Mama into thinking that he was a good God-fearing man.

Well, let me tell you right now that he wasn't. He was a fake. An imposter. He was what Christians call "a wolf in sheep's clothing." "Beware of false prophets, who come to you in sheep's clothing, but inwardly they are ravening wolves." Jesus warned us about these characters in the Gospel of Matthew. I am sure that if Jesus had known Jimmy Ray Walker He would have been talking about him.

The reason Jimmy Ray was able to disguise his "wolfish intentions" was that he was sort of good looking and dripping with charisma. Mainly due to his enchanting personality, most misguided church girls overlooked "the wolf" in him and saw only "the sheep's clothing." So what made him so intoxicating that the women got all giddy inside? I tell you what. He imitated the TV preachers. He acted like a walking, talking, ball of fire TV evangelist just waiting to explode on the scene with his clever and persuasive preaching.

Every Sunday, Jimmy Ray displayed his talent—the ability to be electric and captivating. One smitten church girl, Annabelle Bly, once remarked that Pastor Walker was in his glory (or "glowree" as Southerners pronounce it) when he preached on prosperity and sang this wretched song that he wrote:

The Prosperity Dance by Pastor Jimmy Ray Walker

> *Jesus was poor so we can be rich.*
> *Don't settle for crumbs from the table.*
> *Just name it and claim it and it can be yours.*
> *Declare it if you are able...*
> *Say...*
> *Money comes from the North and the South*
> *From the East and the West, come to me.*
> *Refunds and checks and coupons and wills,*
> *Let the loot from God's throne be your booty.*
> *He's your big Granddaddy. He's your bank in the sky.*
> *He's your slot machine, your lucky lotto guy...*
> *So put the cash in the plate and you'll get a rebate....*
> *Do the Prosperity Dance!*
> *Yes, sir!*
> *Do the Prosperity Dance!*

After holy-hopping around on one foot while crooning the ill-written rubbish, he added one of the corniest things I've ever heard: "And remember folks T.I.T.H.E.S means, *Take it to Him every Sunday!*"

Would you believe that after that lyrical abomination the church would collect some of the biggest offerings of the year? To the best of my recollection, the week after Jimmy Ray made a fool of himself with that awful number, the women at the Wednesday night supper talked about how they could scrimp on grocery money so that they could give a big offering to Jimmy Ray Walker, whom they referred to as —"The Man of God." "The. . . . Man. . . . of . . . God." The way the women said it made it sound like they were talking about Moses, Elijah or some famous healing evangelist on Christian TV and not Jimmy Ray. Truth be told, most of the women had a *serious* crush on him.

Fat Frieda was especially enamored.

Remembering back to that particular Wednesday night supper—the potluck when they served kraut and weenies, creamed potatoes and black-eyed peas, I distinctly recall a conversation that Frieda Plunders was having with Beulah Hulahan:

Tub-o-lard Frieda: Wasn't Pastor just the most anointed you've ever seen him at his appreciation supper, Beulah?

Back Stabbing Beulah: Oh my, yes indeedie, Frieda. And that luscious suit he was wearin'? That navy blue pinstripe? Didn't he look so dad-gum precious?

Tub-o-lard Frieda: I agree, I agree. So dad-gum precious. That wife of his better watch herself. She'd better pick up a little weight, shed those horrible slacks, put on a decent dress and start looking like a pastor's wife or she's liable to find herself in divorce court. Pastors' wives don't need to be wearing pants or bathing suits.

And then, Tub-o-lard Frieda went up to Mama, who was sitting at another table beside the music leader and said, "I just love your new pants outfit, dearie! It makes you look so slim, you should wear it to church every time the doors are open!" she crooned. Not only was Frieda fatter than a tub-o-lard but this statement to Mama revealed that she was also a two-faced liar with a butt bigger than the backside of Birmingham, if you ask me.

I saw the betrayal coming.

Yes. I saw it coming. Mama's troubles with others always came down to one thing—jealousy. Yes, that green-eyed monster was stirring in Frieda and rearing its ugly head on that momentous night. And not only was that jealousy monster's head "ugly" but Frieda's head was ugly too. Frieda had an outdated perm that looked like rats had been sucking on it.

Frieda was fat. Frieda was ugly-haired. Frieda was jealous. And with all of that sin stirring around in her sick soul, Frieda was about to stir up some trouble with the Trustees. Because Frieda could not find anything overtly evil about Mama to complain about, the best she could come up with was Mama's unconventional fashion statements on Wednesday nights when she wore her pants outfits. Back in the day, women wearing pants to church was a controversial issue in some religious circles. I can still hear the legalistic sermons about women wearing pants resounding in my head, sermons that I heard on one of the tapes that Jimmy Ray played by Samuel Hargis Ignatius Theford:

> *Throughout the years, that old devil still tries to destroy mankind through the weakness of a woman just like he did back in the Garden of Eden. Even now, that old devil is whispering to the women, "Do your own thing! Burn your bra! Get a career! Dress like a man!" But I ask you right now, brothers and sisters, is a woman supposed to wear pants? Hell Nope. Women dressing like men is nothing more than perversion from the devil. And not only from THE DEVIL, but from every devil in the lowest pit of the darkest Hell. Here a devil. There a devil. Everywhere a devil-devil. The Bible is crystal clear on the subject. Women are not supposed to wear pants! I'll say it again so you can hear me. Women are not supposed to wear pants! Can I get an amen, brothers and sisters! Can I get a big, fat, holy Amen?*

And so, the week after Jimmy Ray sang his lounge lizard song, the women of the church had to take their focus off Jimmy Ray and put it on children's church matters. It was nearing the end of May, the school year was about to come to a close and there would be a mess of children at loose ends getting on their parents' last nerves. The women of *The Flow* had to get busy and appoint someone to direct Vacation Bible School. Like a fool, Mama offered her services. This action, dear readers, ushered in Mama's season of persecution.

The Flow was an old family church, chock full of old women like Frieda, who had old-fashioned ideas of how a preacher's wife should look and act. Some of the cardinal rules preachers' wives were expected to follow included: *Always wear a dress to church; always be courteous to everyone; always offer to help the women folk in the kitchen.* Any deviation from these unspoken rules would provoke those religious women to make the non-conformist's life pure hell. So when Mama stepped up to the plate to direct Vacation Bible School and showed up at her first organizational meeting with another pants outfit on, Frieda became furious and reported Mama's progressive fashion statement to the Board of Trustees. After Frieda told on Mama, the Trustees sent Mama a letter that requested her presence at their monthly meeting to account for "ongoing fashion improprieties."

Mama's hands were shaking like a leaf when she read that letter. Angry as she could be, she tossed that piece of stationery down on our old kitchen table and hollered, "Shugah, come in here and see what those so called 'good Christians' are up to now!"

When we showed up at the meeting, which was held at the Calhoun's mansion, we were ill-prepared for what transpired. Elder Earl was the first to begin the verbal lynching. "Jimmy Ray," he said in his uppity elder voice, "while we know that you have been very busy with visiting the sick and running the church, we were wondering why you have turned over some of your responsibilities for Vacation Bible School to the little woman who, by the way, showed up in a *pants outfit* at the organizational meeting. *A pants outfit.* We tolerated this indecency when she showed up in pants at the Wednesday night meetings, but wearing pants to a VBS meeting? Really now. Is your salary not sufficient to go out and buy her a wardrobe more fitting for a preacher's wife?"

Fat Frieda chimed in, straining to turn her portly body to face Mama. "We have our standards here, honey, and I fear that the younger women of the congregation think that us Southern women are becoming mannish and trying to step outside the roles that God ordained for us. If I might say so myself, you looked rather severe and unfeminine in that pants outfit. I don't mean to hurt your feelings, and I mean it in the most Christian way possible—the pants were a little tight. Don't you agree with me, Lila Mae?"

"Oh, yes, you are so right, dear," Lila Mae Calhoun replied, "we don't want our husbands distracted from the service of the Lord. Perhaps, Careen, you need one of us to take you under our wings and teach you how to function in your honored role as the first lady of *The Flow*—what do you say? Let us help you."

Mama was speechless, at first.

Jimmy Ray wasn't. Trying not to act offended, he tightened up his jaw and said, "Well…well, I am so glad that you have cared enough to offer your counsel, Lila Mae. And I want to thank the trustees for bringing this to my attention. I assure you that my wife has not taken on any of my duties. And I'm sure with the kind help of her sisters here at *The Flow* that in no time flat Careen will be the perfect model of a preacher's wife. Now if you'll excuse me, ladies and gentlemen, we'll be heading on down the road." And with that parting shot, he grabbed my mama by the elbow and dragged her to the door.

Let me tell you here and now—grabbing Mama in that manner was the wrong thing to do. Jimmy Ray should have known better. He had married a woman with a history of emotional and physical abuse. What was the chance that Mama was going to submit to his coarse treatment?

"Let me go," Mama huffed. "Get your hands off me!" she yelled. "When I divorced Martin McBride, I vowed that I'd never let another man hurt me. God as my witness, Jimmy Ray, you'd better get your grubby hands off of me or you will live to regret it!"

I'm telling you, when I heard her say that, back in the day, I was so proud of her I thought my heart would burst with pride. Just as I was having that feeling, Mama broke away from Jimmy Ray and bolted out the door.

And the race was on. Mama pranced across the room, headed towards the car and was leading by a nose. Jimmy Ray followed close behind, but not before he did something else completely ignorant. He jerked me up from my chair by my elbow and practically dislocated it in the process. As he did, I hit my leg against the dining room table and knocked over Miss Frieda's glass sugar bowl. It hit the floor and shattered into a million tiny pieces. As Frieda stared down at her prized family heirloom, she looked horrified.

"Run, Mama, run!" I thought.

When we were out of the Calhoun's house and sitting in the car, Jimmy Ray and Mama got into a screaming match. "I'm telling you, JR," she said, "I am telling you in no uncertain terms that if you are going to stand back and let those church people mistreat me like that—then I will be taking up for myself. I trusted you!" Mama yelled. "Some preacher you are, getting up in front of your congregation and talking about the love of Jesus and then manhandling your wife just to show off in front of the trustees like that. You are nothing but a damn hypocrite!"

As true as it was—it was the wrong darn thing to say. Being who he was, Jimmy Ray took those words as an invitation to a scrapping match. Underneath that slick preacher persona, Jimmy Ray was nothing but a good old boy with a temper like a wild cat—a brute beast with macho, bigoted, gender-biased evil coursing through his veins.

Jimmy Ray was not going to stand for a woman telling him what to do—Jesus or no Jesus. Male pride was at stake. Suddenly, and without warning, that misogynistic spirit rose up in him and he backhanded Mama with a swift slap—straight across the face. When I screamed in response to his violence, he threw a punch at me, yelled "shut-up" and slammed me into the car window. Almost immediately, a huge bump began to form on my jaw. In the midst of this craziness, I saw Jimmy Ray go at Mama again as he reached over to grab her by the hair on her head and said, "Don't you ever, ever, embarrass me in front of the church people, you Jezebel. From now on, you just sit quietly by my side and shut-the-hell-up. You'd better submit to me or the deacons will have to scrape you off the floor, woman!"

During his pitiful tirade, I saw a clump of Mama's golden locks break off in Jimmy Ray's mean-spirited hand. At first, I just stared at her in disbelief. But then, in a most ghastly state of shock, I happened to look up and see Frieda Plunders standing on the front porch of the Calhoun's house with a huge smile on her fat face.

I honestly don't remember what happened after this. I felt sick to my stomach and then everything went black as the ace of spades. All I remember now is that when I woke up, I was at home on the couch in the living room with a bag of frozen peas on my face. And Mama—she was sitting next to me with her head bandaged.

Full body shiver.

CHAPTER 15

VO5 HAIR AND ALL THAT

AFTER JIMMY RAY ASSAULTED MAMA, she hardened her heart towards that abusive man and I didn't blame her one bit. "I put up with untold crap from your father and I'll be darned if I'm gonna put up with it now," she declared. "I just need to get my bearings and decide if I'm gonna stay or leave."

Apparently, Jimmy Ray knocked all of the love she had left for him right out of her loving heart.

The way I see it, because of all those pop psychology books I read, Jimmy Ray had issues. Severe issues. Having been an addict, Jimmy Ray had this gaping hole in his soul that needed filling—a ravenous need for attention. I don't know why Mama could not see this from the start. "He's just a diamond in the rough," she'd say when I pointed out his flaws. "Nothing that the love of a good woman can't fix." But just like she couldn't fix Martin, I knew that she couldn't fix Jimmy Ray either. Because, as any idiot knows, you can't fix someone who doesn't want to be fixed.

Jimmy Ray thought that he was fine just like he was—arrogance and all. Good gosh, he was cocky. I can still see him in my mind's eye strutting and grinning as he sang that "Prosperity Dance" song. To entertain myself and get back at him for being such an abusive, egotistical jerk, I tapped into my creativity and composed a song to be sung in his honor on Pastor Appreciation Day. This is the same day Mama decided that she wanted a divorce—glory to God.

For those of you who have never been to a Pastor Appreciation Day service, it is an event in which the people of the church recognize and honor their pastors. Depending on which denomination of church you are in, the event can be as simple as holding a meal in honor of the pastor or as elaborate as setting aside a whole week's worth of gift giving, party throwing, and general fawning over the man who is supposed to be a humble servant of the Lord.

In Jimmy Ray's church, the honoring took the form of a singspiration, punctuated by love offerings that began on Sunday morning and ended on Sunday night. On the day that we "appreciated" Jimmy Ray, the Sunday morning service consisted of numerous musical specials and guest speakers who exhorted the congregation to keep supporting the pastor. The evening's festivities were the best part. The festivities included a meal, followed by special testimonies, reading or songs by members selected from the congregation who enthusiastically praised Jimmy for just being the "Charis-maniac" that he was.

It was during this event that I took the opportunity to express how I really felt about Jimmy Ray. Calling on my flair for rhyme, I wrote a song called "The Narcissistic Blues." I begged Mama to get her revenge on Jimmy Ray by embarrassing him in front of God and everybody at his honorary supper.

At first, she looked at me like I was crazy and refused to entertain the idea, but as she mulled it around in that creative brain of hers, I could see the "bad girl" in her rise to the occasion. "It serves him right," she rationalized, "for deceiving me and putting me through hell. He deserves it—him and the whole hypocritical bunch at *The Flow*. Alright then, I'll just put on a show at *The Flow*."

I suppose I could say that the idea to make fun of Jimmy Ray was inspired by the devil, but to say that would not have given credit where credit is due. It really was all my idea. All mine. I had been waiting for a time such as this to humiliate publicly the cocky kook, the man who had abused Mama and me and gotten away with it—and the time had come. The supper was finished. The coffee was poured and the fat ladies of the harem were crowded around the dessert table.

It was time for Mama to sing. I couldn't wait!

After Jed Farley had finished his speech about Jimmy Ray being the most energetic pastor he'd ever met, Mama raised her hand and said that she'd like to honor her husband, Jimmy Ray, with a special song. As those words came out of her mouth I could see the twinkle in his dark eyes, as if he just knew that more praise and adoration was forthcoming. While he was basking in all the man-worship and hoopla, Mama slipped one in on him. She went right over to the microphone, whipped out the words to my song on a sheet of paper that she had kept hidden inside her bra and said: "Right now, in this very room, in front of God and everybody, I feel it's necessary to release this song into the universe as a "tell off" to arrogant pastors everywhere who think of themselves more highly than they ought! Pointed, anointed and easy to remember – it's dedicated to Jimmy Ray Walker…"

Narcissistic Blues

He's got the low-down stinkin'—narcissistic blues
He's got the low-down stinkin'—narcissistic blues
Oh, he wouldn't know if he loved you honey, unless he read it in the news!
Why can't you love me darlin'? You just love yourself
Why can't you love me sweet darlin? You just love, love, love, yourself
You're too blind and so self-centered—
You will surely, surely end up in Hell.
H-E-Double-L, oh yeah…
Well, Jimmy is a haughty guy
A snooty guy with a self-loving flair
Well, I said that Jimmy is a haughty guy
With that greasy, slick VO5 hair.
He is so blind and so self-centered—
He will surely, surely end up in Hell.
Oh, yeah, oh yeah…
He's got the low-down stinkin'—narcissistic blues
He's got the low-down stinkin'—narcissistic blues
Oh, he wouldn't know if he loved you honey, unless he read it in the news!

Lordy be! Mama was gesturing toward Jimmy Ray the entire time she sang. During her dramatics, I swear to high heavens, you could have heard a pin drop in that fellowship hall. That bitter woman let it rip.

After Mama "showed her rear" as Southerners say, she stormed out of the dining hall and dragged me with her. "I suppose that just ended my marriage," she said glibly. "I guess I've put up with so much crap from him that I've gone off my rocker. Lost it. Gone nuttier than a fruit cake." Mama was laughing so hard when she said this; I thought she would burst at the seams.

Living with Jimmy Ray had obviously rattled her cage. Left her one brick shy of a load.

Well, enough about Mama. To change the subject, what did you think about the line in my song about the VO5 hair? I'm still rather proud of it, if I must say so myself!

CHAPTER 16

VENGEANCE IS MINE

SO THERE YOU HAVE IT. Mama and I acted like little *piss ants* at the appreciation supper and I actually thought that we were going to get away with it without a heap of trouble.

I was wrong.

The folks at *The Flow* might have been silent while we were doing our tell-off, but after the song and sermon were over, they sure got their dander up. After the appreciation supper, as Mama and I were on our way to the parking lot ready to get into the car and go—there came three elders and Jimmy Ray busting through the church doors, following us in hot pursuit. "Let's just get into the car Mama," I screamed. "They look like a pack of mad dogs. I don't feel like getting hit again! Mama, Let's go!"

I grabbed hold of her hand and we started running toward the car.

Sometimes Mama is an airhead—the blonde in her, I suppose. She is notorious for not being able to find her keys—for carrying a big bulky purse and losing them among the scads of useless objects that sink to the bottom of her pocketbook. This was one of those times. We would have made it out of there and been miles down the road, if she had been more organized. If she'd only have put the keys in one of those little pockets she would have found them sooner.

But she didn't and that gave the elders and Jimmy Ray just enough time to catch up with us. As they approached the car, I didn't know what to expect. Were they just going to talk to us? Yell at us? Cuss us out? Quote scripture?

What they did was a surprise attack. In one swift movement, they turned to Jimmy Ray, punched him in the belly, and said, "You get in the car with your wife and child and go home and make *believers* out of them. I expect you to get your home *under control* or we will call headquarters and you will never preach or pastor again."

"What the heck did that mean? Get your home *under control?*" Just as the question crossed my mind, Jimmy Ray jumped into the car with us, locked all the doors, cranked the car and tore out of that parking lot. I could see the veins bulging out on his neck and see the fire in his eyes. I knew that something bad was coming, but I couldn't figure out what he was going to do next. He just drove like a bat out of hell through the neighborhood on the way back to our house.

It is a wonder that we were not stopped by the police as fast as we were going. And as fast as the car was going, Jimmy Ray's mouth went faster. The man was quoting every Scripture on submission and headship that he could pull out of that evil brain of his. "Listen woman. Don't you know the Bible says 'the husband is the head of the wife' and that 'wives are supposed to submit to their husbands as they are to the Lord.' And to you, *Miss Smarty Pants*, children are supposed to 'obey their parents in the Lord, for this is right.' Both of you are as stubborn as mules. I'd like to knock both of you in the head and tell God you died!"

Jimmy's voice was escalating. He sounded crazed, like he was on something. The man had flipped. And we were trapped in the car with that savage, spiritual snob. That was the day when I wished that God *was* as mean as the Baptist preacher of my childhood made Him sound. That was the day that I wished that God was still in the Old Testament mindset, and would have sent down plagues, flies, frogs, and fire on Jimmy Ray!

I looked over at Mama; she was shaking like a leaf. I bet she thought that she was going to get a beating when we got home. Seeing Mama all terrified and pale like that made me determined to do something to stop him. Just then, as he was still acting like a fool, he reached over to grab hold of the warm can of Coca-Cola that Mama had left in the car and shouted, "I've got the headache of my life, woman—because of you and your rebellious child. Feels like a shotgun is going off inside my head, but be assured when it passes I will deal with both of you! Now, give me your purse, woman, I need some pills."

And with that said, he grabbed Mama's purse out of her lap and began to rummage through the junk.

"Get your grubby paws out of my purse!" Mama cried, and then she added, "You know you are not supposed to get in a woman's purse! Didn't your mama teach you anything?"

Say what? He was about to beat her brains out and she was thinking about protecting the privacy of her purse?

I'm not entirely sure why purse privacy is so important to women, but it is. Heathen or Christian, we women do not give a man abandoned access to the contents of our handbag. To have a man rummage through your purse feels almost as intrusive as having someone read your mind. Women in my family have been extremely guarded about their pocketbooks for generations and it has been rumored that many a man has had his fingers "cut slap off" as they say in the South, when his angry wife discovered that he was meddling where he clearly did not belong.

"Careen, I've got a splitting headache all of a sudden," he grunted. "It's so bad I can hardly see the road or you—or your sorry excuse for a girl. I've gotta have something to knock out this pain, you hear. I must be having one of those migraines. Where the hell are your painkillers? Your purse is like a black hole. How can you ever find anything in this mess?" His tone of voice was menacing.

"Well, hot shot," Mama said. "I suppose you'll just have to see if you can drive and find the pill bottle at the same time. I'm sure not gonna help you!" She had a sneaky looking smile on her face that clued me into the fact that something was up.

In that instant, I saw Jimmy Ray extract a small plastic bottle from the bottom of her purse, screw off the childproof top, and swig down a handful of pills. All the while, Mama just sat there flashing a grin so wide that she looked like the Cheshire Cat on happy pills.

And why was Mama grinning? I'll tell you why. Mama knew that church girls were not supposed to do it, but she brazenly did it anyway— she mixed different types of pills together in an empty pill container in her purse for her own selfish medicinal convenience. The container held a few of her favorites including vitamins, allergy pills, Ibuprofen and AZO pills. For those of you who do not know about AZO pills, they're small, cranberry-colored pills that ease the discomfort of urinary tract infections. When taken, your urine turns bright orange-red. Women know all about them and they have been known to worship them on occasion because they ease the torment of a burning, churning, bladder infection.

Most certainly, AZO pills are a godsend unless you are a man and unaware that you have taken one and then this becomes a problem. Jimmy Ray had popped what he thought was a handful of Ibuprofen, and proceeded on down the road to our house. His head must have been hurting pretty darn bad because he didn't preach or cuss or hit either of us that night. When we got home, he immediately shut off all the lights, stumbled into the bedroom and plopped himself down on the mattress like a dead man.

Mama told me that the next thing she remembered was the alarm sounding at 6:30 a.m. Apparently, Jimmy Ray's headache was gone but his bladder was screaming for release. So into the bathroom the poor man ran, having forgotten to relieve himself the night before.

All of a sudden, piercing, earsplitting sounds emanated from the bathroom, sounds so loud that the two neighboring counties probably heard them. "Demon of sickness, come out in Jesus' name! Out! Out! Out!" he shouted. "I will live and not die! I will see the goodness of the Lord in the land of the living!"

His thunderous protests rolled throughout the entire house like a scene from the movie *The Exorcist.* And then, after that tacky tirade, Mama and I heard something that sounded like the tongues of toxic church girls:

"She-came-in-on-a-Honda-come-tie-my-bow-tie!"

"Pray for meeeee, Careen!" I heard him scream through the bathroom door. "Something's desperately wrong! Come!" He beckoned. "Come now. Look in the toilet. There's blood in my urine!" he yelled. "Blood! I'm bleeding to death, woman. I'm bleeeeee-ding!"

So, like a good Christian wife, Careen got out of bed and headed straightway into the bathroom to peer into the toilet bowl. "Ah Hah!" she said smugly and folded her arms across her chest. She was quick to recognize that reddish color. Her controlling, abusive husband was not ill; he had just broken the "Sacred Purse Rule." He had swallowed AZO pills instead of Ibuprofen! It served him right—he deserved as good as he got.

And Mama was no fool. Her lips were zipped. She wouldn't have told him what was wrong if her life depended on it. It was too much fun watching him pee red and suffer!

There is an ancient female proverb that goes like this:

"A man who raids a woman's purse will to himself invoke a curse!"

There was no need for Mama and me to worry about getting back at Jimmy Ray. God had it all under control!

Vengeance was His.

CHAPTER 17

BIG PURPLE CHURCH

IT ALL HAPPENED SO FAST—THE appreciation supper, the AZO pills, the bladder crisis and then—divorce number two.

While Jimmy Ray was laid up in the hospital having extensive tests run because of his *colorful* urine, Mama laughed all the way to the attorney's office and filed for divorce. Then, not wanting to waste time, she got on the ball and went house hunting. In less than three days, she found what she was looking for and moved us across town into a charming cottage.

Picking herself up by the bootstraps, Mama told me that she was not going to sit around feeling pitiful like she did when her marriage to my father ended. Instead, she decided to forget all about men for a while and to get a job. I thanked God that she made a practical decision for once. We certainly weren't going to survive very long from trying to live solely on our looks and stunning personalities.

Since the only employment Mama had ever had in her whole married life was working as the pianist at the Covenant Legalist Church, she couldn't afford to be too picky. So, while flipping through the classified ads one Saturday, she came upon an ad for cosmetic sales. She took my advice, called the number, scheduled an interview and wouldn't you know it—she became a new Mimi Makeover consultant.

Mimi Makeup. Could it sound any cornier? When she told me about her new job, I couldn't stop giggling for weeks. I envisioned her all dressed up in her peach colored uniform prancing from door to door trying to sell eye shadow and matching lipstick. But, when I saw how serious she was about trying to make a living and how good she was at selling the stuff, I quickly changed my tune. The money started rolling in, the bills were getting paid and Mama was making over $40,000 a year before we even knew what was happening. It was a miracle! Her gift for gab had eventually paid off. Apparently, her customers loved her dearly because she was friendly and entertaining. I benefited from the whole makeup ordeal too. I got my face done for free and was given plenty of makeup samples. Red, pink, orange, peach—I'll bet I was one of few girls in high school who had more shades of lipstick than they could possibly wear.

Unfortunately, because of the move, we ended up having to change school districts, so I had to start all over in the ninth grade at a different school. Like a typical adolescent, I didn't take this change too well. I fought with Mama about having to leave my old school. She fought back by telling me how ungrateful I was for not understanding her problems. "Like your father used to say: 'everything changes, nothing remains the same.'" Like a smart ass, I reminded her that the saying was not original, that Father had gotten it from that heathen called Buddha. As I would expect from my mother, she told me that I had a choice: Either I could quit sassing or I could go to my room. I chose to quit sassing so I could stay in the living room and watch the *Mary Tyler Moore* show on TV. Mary Tyler Moore—the woman whose theme song included the line "You're gonna make it after all." And if Mary (a middle-aged woman) could make it, why couldn't we?

"But you will not make it," the dark thought nagged. "Maybe you and your Mama will end up in the poor house. Maybe you will end up on welfare or begging some minister to give you canned goods and rice from the church pantry." Those devilish voices kept harassing me, night and day, day and night. Never once did it occur to me that I had a choice as to whether I should entertain them or not. After a few weeks of this torment, it seemed like a foregone conclusion; Mama and I would end up poor as a church mouse.

As sure as I embraced those thoughts, what I feared actually did come upon us. Many months down the road, Mama looked at the checkbook one day and found out that we were broke. Flat broke, I tell you. Poor as Job's turkey. My phantom Father had forgotten to send alimony and child support payments for two straight months, Mama had low sales as the Mimi Makeup Girl and Jimmy Ray—well that ridiculous PH.D wouldn't have given us a crumb. Not knowing exactly what we should do, Mama decided to swallow her pride and go to the church around the block and ask the minister for assistance.

Having to go to a church to ask for help was a humiliating, eye-opening experience. The way the minister looked at us when Mama explained our situation made us feel like the scum of the earth. "Careen," he said, arrogantly, while looking down that ski-jump nose of his, "There is no reason for an able-bodied woman like you to end up coming to a church pantry for help. Surely there are things in your life that you should have done but haven't or else you would not be in this shape. Did you forget to confess the sin in your life? Pay your tithe? Pray for the missionaries? Give to the starving children in Africa? I'll bet if you think long and hard about it you can find some *sin of omission* to blame yourself for."

Good gracious—what an interrogation we had to endure in order to get a few canned goods. But if that didn't beat all—the preacher said that any recipient of charity would be required to attend at least one service at his church within the month. After he said that, Mama looked at him like he had lost his ever-loving mind—and I don't blame her. What committee came up with that insane requirement? First of all, you make someone feel like low-life trash and then you make them pay you back for a few canned goods by demanding that they come to your church? In my humble Alabamian opinion, he needed killin'.

When Mama got over the shock of it all, she reluctantly agreed to the deal. But that wasn't all, there was more. More conditions. The pastor had her sign some dumb form to make sure she'd keep her word. As Mama angrily scribbled her name on the dotted line, the miser went into the storeroom, gathered no more than a dozen cans of pork and beans and meticulously placed them in a cardboard box as if he were packing the crown jewels of England. "This should be more than enough," he grumbled. "And don't forget, I expect to see you and your daughter here within the month to fulfill our agreement, do you understand?" Looking quite stunned, Mama shook her head, took the box and headed toward the door.

We couldn't get home fast enough.

Wanting to make good on her word and to get the church visit out of the way we showed up at *The Purple Palace* the following Sunday. As you might imagine, with a name like that it was no ordinary church.

Mama and I were completely speechless when we entered the building. Almost everything in the church was…well—incredibly purple. For those of you who are not familiar with color symbolism in the religious world, purple is associated with royalty, wealth and opulence, and glory. I suppose that those religious folks wanted us to know that they were a cut above mere mortals.

The purple colors started in the foyer. Light purple on the upper part of the walls. Dark purple near the floor. Purple wall hangings. Purple curtains. Purple flower arrangements. Standing in the midst of this purple haze, our eyes were drawn to the life-size picture of the pastor on the wall. There he was in a purple robe and sash along with matching purple jewelry. We looked around for a cross or a picture of Jesus, but none was in sight, just the lavish purple portrait. The whole egomaniacal representation was designed for folks to think that this "man of God" was royal, important, authoritative, and oh, so very special.

We got the point! He's *The Man!*

So Mama and I were standing there in the foyer, gawking at the picture of *The Man*, when an usher tugged on our arms and pulled us in the direction of the service. Navigating through the sea of purple, we walked through the doors of the sanctuary, hoping that someone had varied the decorating scheme and perhaps blended in some red or green to assuage our nausea, but of course, this wasn't the case. More purple. Purple walls, purple carpet, purple banners, and purple pews. Putrid.

I could walk you through the entire service in all the *monochromatic* details, but it would only bore you. I wasn't even present to the affair. My body was going through the religious rituals, but my mind was elsewhere. Inside I was throwing a hissy fit, because if there is one thing I hate more than heat rash, sinus infection and beef liver, it is those cocky preachers and their spiritual arrogance.

And in the midst of my fit, there came the offering plate. Mama didn't have very much green money, but what she did have would have clashed terribly with the purple plate, so she let it pass right on by. But this didn't bother the preacher. When he saw several other people were not giving—he sent the plate around again.

So there we were, watching the offering plates circulate around and around the church. With all of that continuous motion (coupled with the fact that I had not had a bite to eat the whole day) I was getting really dizzy. In an effort to steady myself, I grabbed hold of the purple pew in front of me, and when I did—I stumbled and fell sideways bumping right into a kindly looking black woman in her sixties named Essie. Instead of chastising me, the sweet saint helped to steady me on my feet. Although embarrassed, I thanked her for her kindness. Then, she patted me tenderly on the arm and whispered, "Don't worry, *Baby Doll*, God don't like this purple stuff either. I just came because I'm payin' the preacher back for giving me a dad-gum case of Pork and Beans."

I started laughing so hard, I thought that the elders were going to have to carry me out of the place. Come to find out, Essie was in the same bad financial condition as Mama and I were. From what she told me, the preacher had treated her the same way he had treated my Mama and me when we came to the church for help. The Purple Palace truly was no respecter of persons. The pastor and his staff treated every financially destitute person in the same degrading manner. Brood of vipers!

Unbeknownst to me at that time, there was a reason that I met Essie at that big purple church. Like the Bible says (in the ever popular King James version—the version that some misguided folks believe is the only version you should read), "And we know that all things work together for good to them that love God, to them who are the called according to His purpose."

It would not be too long before Essie would come into my life again and be "*working for my good.*" But, before that season could come to pass, I had to be prepared to receive the goodness.

And sometimes preparation is painful.

Chapter 18

Put on Your Big Girl Panties and Deal With it!

Not many months after we left that ceremony at the Big Purple Church and got back on our feet financially, the divorce was final. With Jimmy Ray completely out of our lives, I felt a great sense of relief and I sure was hoping that Mama did too.

With that chapter of our lives coming to a close, I was ready to forget all about marriages and divorces and be a teenager. I wanted to do things that normal teens did like date, go to slumber parties, and play spin the bottle. I wanted to do things—daring things like stay out past curfew and French kiss a boy on the front porch.

Yes. I was more than ready to engage life with my youth and raging hormones, but the problem was—I didn't have a life of my own. Mama had spent her life making my father, Jimmy Ray, and religion the center of her world and I had spent my life making Mama the center of mine. As much as I hated to admit it, it was becoming as plain as the nose on my face: I was codependent. And if I had died as a young adult (as the joke goes), the last thing I would have seen is *Mama's* life flash before my eyes.

Go ahead and laugh, but it was not a laughing matter. Looking back on my relationship with Mama, I had in many ways acted like her Mama. I had taken care of her during her marital troubles. I had taken care of her during her great depression. It's not that she was unworthy of this care, but the last time I could remember really being a child was—well, I couldn't remember. And that was the problem. Unknowingly, my Mama had robbed me of my childhood and of the friendships I could have made if I had not been reared to be a little grown-up.

As you know now, I'd been so caught up with Mama and the family's problems that I'd gone through most of my childhood with nothing more than mere acquaintances—except for Clementine who was, well, you know—dreadful, sorry. Come to think of it, I couldn't think of anyone whom I knew really well, or regretfully, anyone who really knew me. Down in the depths of my heart, I still felt like a child left out in the rain...

> *The thunder rolls in this restless heart*
> *And my desperate eyes crying all I've got*
> *Can't believe your leaving brought so much pain*
> *And I feel like a child left out in the rain...*
> *There's a bitter wind blowing through my soul*
> *I beg it to leave me but it won't let go*
> *Can't believe your leaving brought so much pain*
> *And I feel like a child left out in the rain...*

Every once in a while, I'd try to talk to Mama about my friendlessness, my loneliness and my pain, but she couldn't keep her mind off herself long enough to help me with my problems. As long as I was there for her as a friend, I was in her good graces. The moment I expressed my own needs she blamed me for having any.

The optimism I felt about Mama getting over Jimmy Ray quickly faded when we had been away from him for a couple months. She began thereafter to lose the high of having escaped like a bird from the snare of a fowler and, once again, started slipping into her familiar depression. Like a dog that returns to his vomit, those dark suffocating spirits returned to our house. Mama's moods started slipping and I knew it was only a matter of time before she'd take to her bed.

Instead of nursing her depression, I decided it was time to put my foot down and give her a piece of my mind. Jerk a knot in her tail. Granted, she had suffered through two terrible marriages and had plenty to be miserable about, but did that mean that she had to wallow in it for the rest of her life? What she needed was a good talking to. And like it or not, I was going to give her one.

One night when she wasn't feeling too low, it dawned on me—turnabout is fair play, so I'd initiate one of our mother-daughter talks. So I went into the kitchen and pulled two Wedgwood cups out of the china cabinet. "Mama," I said confidently, "it's time for you and me to have one of our girls' nights again. I'm gonna tell you what's on my heart and you are gonna tell me what's on yours."

So, like a good little church girl, I poured a cup of coffee for Mama and waited for her to come and sit next to me on the couch.

"Mama," I said, taking a deep breath of courage, "I was thinking that this year I need to quit staying at home so much and branch out a little and get a social life. It's not normal for someone my age to be alone so much. Don't you think that I need to be having some friends and going out on dates and enjoying myself?"

"Well, Maggie," she said (totally missing the point), "I suppose you could improve your social life a bit. Would you want me to enroll you in charm school when we get back on our feet? You could use a little poise. You've always been a little *socially awkward*."

Socially Awkward? Already, Mama was treading on thin ice. Telling me that I was socially awkward was not the way to start off a conversation. My dander was rising up and I had not even added the cream and sugar to my cup of coffee. I may have been raised like a little grown up but there was a teenager inside just itching to *rebel*. A teenager wanting to get up in her face and tell her that she could "kiss my butt and call me Rudy."

"I don't think charm school is the answer." I said, constraining my anger. "What I mean is that instead of sitting here in the house talking to you every night, *I* need to be out with people my age having fun. *I* am a teenager for God's sakes. And *you*, Mama, *you* are a middle aged woman. *You* need to be making friends with people *your* age, getting on with *your* life and not depending on *me* so much."

"What are you saying, Maggie? Are you trying to insinuate that I am not good company? That I'm boring? That I'm a burden to you? Did I raise you or did you raise me? Have you been reading Dear Abby? Keep up this nonsense and I'll cancel your birth certificate. Oh, God, oh God, oh God…your reminding me of my mama today," she said while pacing up and down. "I couldn't talk to her either. It was always as if she was in her own little world thinking about what made her happy. I remember trying to tell her what happened to me with Uncle Ebert. . . ."

"Oh, no," I thought to myself, "She did it again." She turned the conversation back around to focus on her and I had to hear one of her stories about some demented uncle named Ebert who was a weirdo that nobody seemed to like. As she sipped on her cup of coffee, she jumped right into her story, completely ignoring what I had just said to her.

"I had always been a good girl, Maggie." She clicked the spoon against the side of the cup with more than a hint of anger. "You know how I feared Papa. I would have never done anything to upset or disappoint him. But just this one time, this one dad-gum time, I decided to disobey…"

"For what, Mama," I interjected.

"For making me stay home on a Friday evening when he had to be out working. He told me I had to stay home and tend to the sickly baby goat. There had been a litter that spring. Josie was the runt. I loved the goat, don't get me wrong. I didn't want anything to happen to it, but I felt so blazing mad. I'd wanted to go to the square dance at my friend Sarah Beth's farm. Sarah Beth Taylor, that is, the most popular girl in school. She had all the good friends, all the good parties and all the good clothes. When she presented me with a real store-bought invitation to the dance, I felt like someone finally thought I was important. So, with a sick goat or not—I was determined to go."

"Oh, goodness, gracious," I sighed, giving Mama the response I thought she wanted.

"So I fed Josie just like Papa asked. I gave her fresh water and put her on a soft pallet near the fireplace. Then, feeling as guilty as a kid caught in a cookie jar does, I got myself dressed in a snazzy outfit and headed out the door. I was defiantly on my way to the square dance at the old Palmer farm to meet Sarah Beth and her friends when I noticed Uncle Ebert up ahead who was walking down the road toward me. From a distance, I could see that he wasn't walking right. He was trying to walk a straight line in front of him but he kept swerving to the left and to the right. I remember that dusky evening very well; I could hear the croaking of the frogs and the chirping of crickets as his heavy feet thudded down that dusty road. I even remember what he was wearing: A brown hat with a reddish shirt that looked like it hadn't been washed in weeks' worth of Sunday's and, black, ugly boots with those heavy rounded toes. Uncle Ebert wasn't drunk enough to fall, but drunk as a skunk, nevertheless. I could tell that he was having a hard time just keeping himself steady. He had a strange look on his face, as if he was up to no good, as he approached me on the road. I tried my best to get around him, but he blocked my path with his burly body. As he came up against me with his dirty, smelly self, I could feel the heat from his loins through his trousers…"

Just as Mama was getting into the heart of the story, I even surprised myself by jumping up from the couch in a fit and shouting, "There you go. . . . *you* have done it again! *You* have turned this conversation around and made it all about you! How *do* you *do* that *every time*? Every blessed time *you* make it about *you*." And just as that came out of my mouth I began to get a tight feeling in my chest like my heart was going to burst.

"I cannot handle hearing these stories, Mama. Don't you understand?" I was still screaming. "I love you, but I can't bear your burdens anymore. It's making me sick. You are a grown woman. Why can't you just *put on your big girl panties and deal with it?*"

I anticipated the worst from her after having said that.

Mama, however, just sat there staring at me like I didn't have the sense God gave a goose. Obviously, she didn't get it. She didn't get that she was being as selfish as they come in regards to her only daughter and my needs. She was not sympathetic towards me at all. In fact, she had a smug, mean look on her face.

"Well, well," she hissed, "I thought we were going to have a *nice little chat* and drink our coffee. And you start in on me with this? I didn't count on you *ruining my night*!"

"*Your night*? What? Is your name written on this night? Oh, get your mind off yourself for one minute and listen to *me!* To *me, me, me !*" I shouted. "I swear to God, Mama, you're enough to make a preacher cuss and piss off the Pope!"

Abandoning my usually restrained self, I had *really* cut loose on her. It was one of those times when your mouth just keeps going and you're saying things you've wanted to say for years. You know you shouldn't continue, but it feels so darn good to be standing up for yourself that you just don't want to quit.

Yep, it was one of those times.

When I had finally finished my wonderful tell off, she turned to look at me face-to-face and square in the eyes and shook her finger in my face and yelled, "Keep this up and you'd better give your heart to Jesus, 'cause your butt will be mine! I just wish to God I'd never bought you those silly self-help pop-psychology paperbacks at that yard sale. You've been doing this amateur psychoanalysis bunk ever since. Sometimes you sound like a walking psycho-dictionary. And you know, *little Missy*, I don't have to put up with this crap. You ain't got no more chance than a *kerosene cat in Hell with gasoline drawers on* in making me feel guilty for your pity party."

When her tirade ended, my hands were shaking like a leaf. I had finally done it. Broken the unspoken Southern rule: *You don't confront Mama.* But little good my fit did. My words fell on her deaf ears. It was no use at all. It was crystal clear to me that the only feelings and thoughts that mattered to her were hers, not mine.

Gone were the days of lighthearted times at the Woolworth's store.

With the passing of time, Mama was becoming more serious and bitter. I finally figured out that if I were to have any relationship at all with that woman, I'd have to guard my heart or I'd get a guilt trip laid on me as thick as mud. If I were going to have any kind of life of my own, *I'd* just have to *put on my big girl panties and deal with it.*

But I couldn't.

CHAPTER 19

NO PEACE FOR THE WICKED

AFTER THAT CONFRONTATION, MAMA ACTED strangely toward me for the next few months. She was hot, then cold, then hot, then cold. Her mood swings were enough to make a preacher cuss. I didn't know from one minute to the next if I'd be getting the sugar cube or the vinegar, the saint or the sinner. She kept me off balance and fearful. I kept dancing around her moods trying to please her, but to no avail.

Something bad had happened to her personality since her divorce from my father. Something that could best be explained in spiritual terms. I didn't know what it was then, but I know now that it was *bitterness*. That old generational curse was having its evil way in our broken home by dividing the two church girls who used to be the closest—Mama and me. And of course, I blamed it on Mama—she let *that* demon in the door when she refused to forgive her sister, Justine.

Aunt Justine. Gosh, how I missed her. Not only *her*, but The Club, the money, and the manicures with the peach-colored nail polish. The last time I spent time with my aunt in Mountain Brook, Mama decided to cut my visit short. She decided to come and get me because she wanted to take me to the yearly Friends of the Library festival.

I remember the day well.

Justine was finishing her fourth martini when the phone rang. She was acting tipsy.

"Yellow," she laughed into the receiver. "*Yellooooo?*"

Mama didn't think Justine was funny. And she let it be known in no uncertain terms. "What in Sam Hill do you mean answering the phone like a drunk?" Mama snapped. "I trusted you with my daughter's care and now you are three sheets to the wind? *God ought to kick your butt*! But since God is not there to do it, I guess I'll have to come over and do it myself. Get her ready, Justine. I'm coming to get Maggie and take her to a festival at our town library this evening. Have her ready when I get there, no *ifs, ands* or *buts*. By the way, Sis, how many drinks have you had today? Three? Four? Ten?"

"Now, wait a minute," Justine replied. "Are you implying that I'm an alcoholic? I'll have you know that I'm completely sober. Listen: I slit the sheet, the sheet I slit upon the slitted sheet I shit." Justine started laughing uproariously again.

"Justine...you're as drunk as *Cooter Brown*. I'm coming to get Maggie."

"Honest-slee," Justine slurred, "You can't just come and take her home. We were planning to go out to supper tonight and then to The Club. You're always thinking of *number one*, sis. Come on, girl. Think of your daughter for a change. Sheez having a ball."

"*Me*. . . always thinking of number one," Mama howled. "Ha! If that doesn't beat all. I'm not the one who ran out on her baby sister when the going got rough at home. You were just interested in making sure that your life was hunky-dory. I don't have to listen to your drunken crap. I'm coming to get Maggie and you'd *better* have her bags packed. Thank God I called."

"Give it up, Careen. Why don't you just forgive, forget and give it up? You can thank your *God* or whomever you want, but she's not going with you tonight, Careen. So you'd better sit your self-righteous butt down on that thrift store sofa of yours and watch yourself some TV this evening. To tell the truth and shame the devil, she's going with me to The Club."

I do declare...when Aunt Justine had insinuated that Mama shopped at the thrift store—well, that went over about as good as a turd in a punch bowl. Because Mama felt insecure as a parent, she immediately got in her car and drove ninety miles an hour from Homewood to Mountain Brook. When she arrived at Justine's and saw that her sister had already passed out on her special-ordered sofa, she told me in no uncertain terms to *get in the car.*

"Get in this car right now, *little Missy.* You should have called and told me that Justine was out of it! She looks like she's been rode hard and put up wet."

By the crazed looked she had on her face, I was too scared to protest. I grabbed my things and did just as she asked. During that long car ride home, I got to hear Mama talk about what had just transpired between her and Justine until I thought I would go crazy. And because of Mama's ugly grudge, that's the last I saw of Auntie J until Nana's (my mama's mama) funeral several weeks later.

I remember it well.

By the time we all reunited at the funeral home to say goodbye to Nana, the sisters *still* had their panties in a wad. Their anger surfaced again when they were peering into the casket:

"I never thought that she'd die suddenly with an aneurism; I guess I thought she'd live forever. That mortician sure did a good job though, doesn't she look *natural*?" Justine sighed.

"Natural? You have got to be kidding. About as natural as a wax mannequin," Mama replied.

"What are you saying that for?"

"Because she's as *painted* as a two-bit whore and as *bloated* as a water balloon."

"Bloated?"

"You heard me—*bloated.* Maybe it's just the color of her blouse that is making her look like a blimp! Tell me, Justine, when in a month of Sunday's did Mother ever like perky pink?"

"Well, I never! If you think that the blouse is not a good color for her then you should have been here to pick out an outfit yourself. But, no-ooo, you were too busy picking out your own outfit for the funeral to be concerned with how Mother looked. And another thing. You know that Mama was self-conscious about her big, puffy hands. You know that she did not want her big manly hands showing. You should have put some little lacy blanket over those huge hands. I swan! You have not got the sense you were born with!"

"You know, Justine, maybe there was a reason that Mama's brain just up and *exploded* a couple of days ago. Maybe she just asked the good Lord to take her home to Glory to get away from the likes of *you!*" Mama had to get the last word in.

And believe it or not, dear readers, this dainty little dialogue took place in front of the coffin with dozens of onlookers. I was standing right behind them in the viewing line and was so embarrassed that I just wanted to disappear. I had so hoped that their mother's death would have been the tragedy that would make them want to put their differences behind them, not only for their sake, but for my sake too. You see, from my point of view, if they continued this feuding and fussing, Mama would have harbored another offense and would have prevented me from spending summers with Aunt Justine.

Just as I had that thought, Mama turned to me in the line and said, "And you can forget all about going to see Auntie Justine this summer. No daughter of mine is going to have anything to do with a sister of mine who talks to me like that. And don't you go giving me that sad hound dog look!"

After the funeral, it went from bad to worse. The sisters continued to have it out at the reception.

"Chicken wings at a funeral reception? Everyone knows that you *do not* have chicken wings at a funeral reception," Justine complained. "You can't expect a bunch of proper Southern women to pick up chicken wings with their bare hands and eat them like barbarians at a picnic. This had to be your idea, Careen. On a divorcee's salary, I'm sure you are still always trying to cut corners."

"I've had about enough of you and your sass, Justine," Mama snapped. "If you say one more smart-ass thing, I'm gonna tell everybody that you shave your upper lip and keep a razor in your fancy Mercedes just in case your five o'clock shadow appears."

"You wouldn't dare."

"Try me, sis."

"If this is the way you're going to be, I just might just as well leave," Justine huffed.

"Well kiss my butt and call me Rudy," Mama yelled.

And there you have it. The rift that began a whole year of silence between the sisters and kept that darn root of bitterness growing like a weed among the women in our family.

But the bitterness didn't start with Mama and Justine; it started with that *dead woman* wearing that putrid pink blouse who was lying in the casket:

Their mother, my grandmother, Mary Rose--whom I called, "Nutty Nana."

As long as I can remember, Nana was referred to as the "*woman who was mental*" by the family. As long as I knew her, she acted unstable and mad at the world. I never knew what was going to set her off so I tried not to cross her. Mama had warned me about not getting her dander up. And to emphasize the point she began telling me about how Nana handled discipline back in Mama's day. "Maggie," Mama said, "Don't you ever cross her and whatever you do—don't, (and I mean *don't*) dirty up her house. If you do, you're liable to end up with the same kind of harms that I got as a child—licks on your buttocks with a wooden spoon, swats on your legs with a fly swatter, whelps on your back from a razor strap, or bruises on your arms from a wooden hair brush that Nana can swing with sharp precision. So, *don't* dirty up her house."

Having been given those painful examples, you can betcha that I tried my best not to inflame her temper whenever Mama and I went to visit. But one horrible weekend, when we were at her farm in Sylacauga, Nana flew into a rage over what I am about to tell you and ended up committing a deadly sin which landed her in *The Haven of Peace*, a private psychiatric facility. And I do mean *deadly*.

Using piss poor judgment, Mama mistakenly thought that her mother might like to have a puppy to keep her company since she was alone so much of the time after my grandfather died. So, on our way to her house, we stopped by a breeder and bought Nana the cutest little Chihuahua you have ever seen. Its head looked as round as an apple and his eyes were as big as his little head. He was so precious—and only about six weeks old. "This little guy will be a lot of company for Nana," Mama told me. We were both excited about giving her the dog and could never have anticipated the tragedy that was going to take place that afternoon.

In spite of our good intentions and much to our disappointment, Nana was *not* happy when we brought the pup through her door. She immediately threw a fit and said that she "was not going to be the one to take care of a stupid animal with all she had to do around the house."

"Oh, Mama," Careen said, "Look how cute he is. Just give him a chance. I'm sure that in no time at all you and he will end up as best buddies."

"Let me tell you something," Nana replied, "As cute as he is, if he messes on my floor, some *heads are gonna roll*."

Well, not thinking that Nana meant this *literally*, we assured her that we would try to keep an eye on the puppy. We also told her that if she decided that she didn't want the puppy that we would take him home with us and keep him ourselves. So, there we were at Nana's with a few hours to kill before we headed home and feeling sorely disappointed that Nana had spurned our gift. I decided that I didn't want to stay in the kitchen with the grownups any longer so I took the puppy and went into the living room to watch TV.

I kept remembering what Nana said about being careful and not letting the puppy do his business on the rug, so I held him in my lap the entire time as I sat and watched reruns of *I Love Lucy*. But then, during one of the commercial breaks, I noticed that the puppy was asleep, so I laid him on the couch and went outside to pick a couple of green apples off the tree in Nana's front yard. Regrettably, I lost track of time, stayed outside too long and . . . . That's when *it* happened.

When Nana walked into the living room and saw that the puppy had messed on her new couch—she went berserk. Off her rocker. Crazy mad. In a violent rage, she yelled for me to come inside and "get the *damn* dog off her *damn* couch." And since I was becoming all freaked out and frightened from her angry outburst, I yelled back at her and that just made matters even worse.

Then, before I could get to the poor puppy, Nana ran over to the couch, grabbed the little Chihuahua by the scruff of his neck and headed outside to the back yard. In a panic, I dropped my apples and ran after her screaming as loud as I could.

"No, Nana, give *me* the puppy…give him to *me*!"

I didn't know exactly what she had in mind, but I knew it wasn't good. As long as I could remember, that woman always had a temperament that would make Pharaoh seem like a Girl Scout.

Just as I made it to the screen door on my way to the back yard, she plopped the poor pup up on top of the tree stump in the back yard, yanked the axe out of a groove in the bark, raised it high above her head and. . .

And this is where it got all weird and fuzzy in my memory.

I do remember what happened next seemed like it was happening in slow motion. Nana brought that cleaver down on the animal's neck with such force, it's a wonder she didn't split the stump in the process. And then there was blood. Bright, red blood everywhere. On Nana. On the puppy. On the stump. On the grass. And when I looked down at my clothes, it had spattered on me, too.

This was the day Nana ended up in *The Haven of Peace*. But she *never* found peace—no, never. Not even with the five different kinds of drugs the doctors gave her *or* the five rounds of shock treatments she received. She never found peace because, as we all know; *there is no peace for the wicked. But the wicked are like the troubled sea, when it cannot rest, whose waters cast up mire and dirt. There is no peace, saith my God, for the wicked.*

Chapter 20

The Appointed Time

WHEN I WAS A CHILD, I was fascinated by my parents' camera. It was an impressive instrument, but hard to operate for a six-year-old with delicate hands. When my folks and I would vacation in the Carolina's, I would beg to use it so that I could take photographs of the ocean. When Mama would finally give into my insistent pleas, I would proceed in my exuberance to capture the grandeur of the billowy waves against the sun-washed sky. But no matter how hard I tried, my small hands and tiny fingers could not coordinate the lenses and levers to bring the scenes into focus. Try after try after try, the results were always the same when I took a picture—cloudy, unfocused depictions of the sea and sky that looked like nothing more than misty, dark, phantasmal images distorted by illusion.

Even though those days are long past, I look back at them now and liken that experience with the shadowy imagery to the struggle that I had trying to understand the wounding of my childhood. Martin was remote and detached. Mama was intrusive and demanding. Between trying to attach to my father and trying to detach from my mother, I was all alone.

I thought about these things after I stood up to Mama and did my tell-off. After I confronted Mama and she told me to *"put on my big girl panties and deal with it,"* I was devastated. During that season of our lives, Mama was incapable of seeing me as a real person with wants and needs of my own.

In the aftermath of that mother-daughter skirmish, I realized that at that season in her life, Mama was totally self-absorbed. I was tired of listening to her pitiful stories about her failed marriage and her wretched puppy-killing mother. I was exhausted from feeling the weight and the sting of her pain. I began to wonder if there was anyone in the world who would ever care enough about me to come alongside and help bind *my* wounds and carry *my* burdens.

Even though I knew that Mama did not mean to hurt me by compulsively sharing her personal problems, the truth was that Mama was hurting me with her selfishness and, somehow, I had to get some of my needs met and lighten my load.

Not knowing what to do about this problem, I went into my bedroom and lay across my bed. I thought about my choices. I could continue living with a woman who obviously had nothing to give or I could do something entirely dramatic and kill myself. The first choice was not appealing but as to the second—the church told me that suicide is a sin and even *church girls* who do it go to Hell. Were there any other options, I wondered?

And then a thought came to me.

Aunt Justine! Why couldn't I go and live with Aunt Justine in Mountain Brook? If by some chance I could end up with Aunt Justine in Mountain Brook, Mama would just kill over from jealousy because she had always coveted to be at the top of a social hierarchy.

I wondered if somehow I could get in touch with my aunt and convince her to come to my rescue. As fragile as I felt at that season in my life, I sensed that I was just a fit away from ending up in the Funny Farm with the people who drool and murmur to themselves about bugs crawling on their skin or Martians sending poisonous fumes through the air conditioning vents. *Insanity* would be my destiny unless I could get a break from Mama's neediness.

I needed a breakthrough.

So, in a flurry of emotion, I rushed to the phone to dial Aunt Justine's number. But just as I put my fingers to the phone, there came a familiar interruption. It was Mama knocking on my door calling out to me, "Maggie, are you in there?" In a panic, I slammed down the receiver and yelled, "What do you want now, Mama?"

Surprisingly, Mama ignored my sass and continued, "Maggie, we have to talk". Defensive about the invitation, I snapped at her. "We do not have to talk. I am tired of talking. That's all we do is *talk, talk, talk*. I am going to go to bed now. Go away."

Even with my unrestrained rudeness, she persisted, "Maggie, I said we need to talk and you need to come into the living room and sit down, now." Her voice was insistent and firm.

I jarred back at her. "Mama, I have to get some sleep and I'm going to bed. *Goodnight.*"

"Maggie," she screamed, pounding ever harder, "I said come to the living room, young lady, and sit down. Now, *right now!*" And with that, I could hear that she burst into tears. Feeling guilty as usual, I opened my bedroom door. By the look on her face, I could tell that there was something definitely wrong with her that was out of the ordinary. I got up out of bed and went into the living room.

"Sit down, Mary Margaret McBride!" Mama yelled at the top of her voice.

It was really serious when Mama used three of my names.

I sat.

"Maggie, I don't know how to tell you this, so I'm just gonna come out and say it: Ellen called."

"Ellen?"

"Yes, Ellen."

"Father's Ellen?"

"Yes, Martin's ugly Ellen."

"And so?"

"Bad news, Maggie. Bad news. Ellen told me that your father was taken by ambulance to the hospital and that….." Her voice trailed off into a whimper.

"And that ……what? What happened, Mama?" I asked, as my heart flipped a beat.

"His *heart*," she answered me. "Your father…"

"Is *dead*? Is *dead!*" I screamed. "Is he *dead?*"

"No, he is not dead *yet*, but they don't think that he will make it through the night."

I blinked, I swallowed, and then my body felt weak like a limp washrag. Denial, anger, and grief moved through me like a shock wave. How could fate be this cruel? This wasn't supposed to happen. He wasn't supposed to *die* before we reconciled. He wasn't supposed to die before I got my happy ending and he changed into the warm, loving daddy he was supposed to have been all along. Surely this is a mistake, I thought.

I was only seventeen and I was going to lose the father I never had? Like the members of the charismatic church had taught me—I could name it and claim it—he was *not* going to die and this was *not* happening.

I looked at Mama. She was just standing there weeping as hard as she did the day that Father told her that he was leaving her for ugly Ellen. I'd never seen someone so undone. A mixture of anger and sorrow flickered across her face. Full of pity, I (once again) forgot about *my* grief and reached for her hand. As she felt me touch her, she closed her trembling fingers around mine.

And there we were once again—two world-weary church girls agonizing over the man who had spurned and rejected both of us so long ago. Two jaded church girls lamenting over the man who walked out on us and made a new life with (butt-ugly) Ellen. Ellen, the who women was not just unattractive but uglier than a bucket full of armpits. Ellen, the wicked mistress who was so ugly that her pillow cried at night.

Sitting next to Mama, who was not ugly in any shape, form or fashion, I nestled my head against her chest. A window above the sofa let in the evening sun that was peacefully drifting below the horizon. Its streams of red and gold shone through the cherry tree in our front yard. In those fearful minutes of uncertainly, I realized that once again I was having that feeling I didn't like…

Fear.

Mama and I held each other's hand for what seemed like an eternity while sitting on that worn, old sofa. It was during those moments when a passage from the Bible from the book of Ecclesiastes came to my mind:

> *To everything there is a season,*
> *and a time to every purpose under the heaven:*
> *a time to be born, and a time to die…*

Was it my father's appointed time, I wondered?

Would my father go to his grave while he had unfinished business with his only daughter?

CHAPTER 21

ROUGH DAY

IT WAS MIDSUMMER WHEN MY father passed away and hotter than a two-dollar whore on the 4th of July. Summers in Alabama could be brutal—sizzling like a juicy sausage in a cast iron skillet. It seemed that everything in the city conspired to make us church girls sweat. Even the dad-gum air conditioner was on the blink at the funeral home. And my late father—death didn't do him any favors. Looking worse for the wear, he was ghastly—like a glistening, gooey mannequin who was lying inside that cheap casket Ellen had purchased.

So there we were—Ellen, Mama, Justine and me. All together. In one room. At the funeral. I'm sure we looked quite comical flapping those tacky cardboard fans back and forth. At ninety-eight degrees, we were *hot* and we were *desperate*. Everyone knows that no matter how sad a Southern girl gets, she still has to look pretty, even in the midst of a good cry. This being the case, we girls were *desperate* to keep the mascara from running down our faces and ruining our classic, little, black, Audrey Hepburn dresses. There's nothing worse than dark spidery streaks on the rosy cheeks of a good church girl.

As we made our way down the viewing line, we noticed Ellen standing near the casket—snorting and blowing into a pink hanky as she wiped that pudgy nose of hers. Mama and Justine looked in her direction, pursed their lips and scowled—not really trying to hide their displeasure at all.

And though our very presence must have been unnerving to the woman, Ellen mustered up a pleasantry.

"Thank y'all for coming. I know it must have been hard for you to come here and pay your respects and all," she said to the three of us in a whiny, pinched voice, while harking back snot as she stood in front of the coffin.

"How dare she patronize us in our grief," I thought to myself. "We are his *real* family."

Then, forgetting for just a moment how much Mama despised her, Ellen reached out to put her hand on my mother's shoulder in a gesture of consolation. Typical for Mama, not able to forgive or forget, she flinched and drew back a nub, letting Ellen know that she was dirt beneath her feet in the demeaning way that only Southern women have perfected. Meanwhile, Aunt Justine stood idly by just waiting for her opportunity to make a statement. Even bickering sisters could be on the same side when the adulteress was present.

No, we weren't invited. Not a one of us. But what kind of tacky woman was going to throw my Father's *real* family out of the funeral home? Certainly not Ellen. She was outnumbered three to one by us. Besides, half of UAB was present, watching us—a good incentive to keep lady-like. That poor Ellen woman. Our presence made her so confused and upset, she looked as nervous as a whore in church with a twenty-dollar bill.

The devil in me was enjoying her anxiety, so I just stood there gawking at the woman who stole my father many moons ago and feeling as cold inside toward her as an ice cube. In my humble estimation, after all the years that had passed between stealing my father and the present funeral, Ellen hadn't changed a bit. To me, the gal was still so ugly that her own dogs tried to keep her hidden under the porch.

I looked at her. Then, I looked at Mama. Then, back at her. Then, back at Mama. Even someone as blind as a bat could see that there was no comparison. Mama was head and shoulders above that woman. Besides being ugly as homemade sin, Ellen couldn't even plan a decent funeral. Instead of doing the proper thing and planning a traditional Irish wake that would have been in keeping with Father's heritage, Ellen planned a traditional Southern funeral.

If my father had known that the funeral would have included prayers, hymns and sermons, it would have made him turn over in his casket. He was an agnostic history professor, for goodness sakes. Leaving the world and remaining true to his heritage would have been important to him. No prayers. No hymns. No God. That's what father would have wanted. Just a good old-fashioned cremation before burning in Hell.

After what seemed like minutes on end of senseless mingling, it was time for the funeral to begin. Though we shouldn't have, Mama, Justine and I sat brazenly on the second row eying the flowers that came from God only knows where. For a short while, it seemed as if we were going to get through one of the worst days of our lives without a bunch of hissy fits. But, "honey child," as Mama used to say, this was a premature conclusion.

Just when it seemed that everyone was behaving themselves, Justine outdid it. She made a scene. The lush pulled a silver flask out of her purse and took a swig of brandy in front of God and everybody. When Mama saw it and started to chastise her, Justine opened her big mouth and started whispering loudly…

"Why the hell did that Ellen woman hire an organ player? Your father never liked the organ. He said it reminded him of church and we all know that man didn't *like church*. And even though he was a heathen and should have believed in our dear Lord and Savior Jesus Christ, Ellen should have respected Martin enough to uphold his heathen heritage."

"Shush," Mama said. "Don't go making fools out of us here, ya hear?"

"Fools?" Justine hissed. "It seems to me that the woman already made fools out of us—taking off with your husband and all while you were still married. How foolish can you get?"

"Aunt Justine, please! Not so loud," I said under my breath. "You're embarrassing me! Do you want to make trouble in front of Ellen's people? They'll think that Father left us for a good reason, that we're nothing but white trash."

"Don't you be calling me white trash!" Mama snapped. "Just because some *hussy* stole my husband doesn't mean that I'm white trash!"

"She wasn't calling you white trash," Justine interjected, coming to my rescue.

"Now Justine, don't you be calling me down in front of my daughter," Mama said.

But Mama said this way too loud, causing ugly Ellen to turn clear around in her seat and give Mama the evil eye. Mama responded, "Don't you go giving me the evil eye you *home wrecker.*"

And this, she said without regard to the others in the room who were listening to our family feud. Just when I thought the tempers were going to rise to intolerable portions, the service started. The music began. At the back of the room I heard what I thought sounded like bagpipes. Listening closer, yes, it was bagpipes. But not live bagpipes. It was a cheesy recording of The Lawrence Welk Orchestra playing a rendition of "Beulah Land." What was next? Bobby and Sissy dancing to the Beer Barrel Polka at the reception?

Just as this thought drifted into my head, the preacher began the eulogy. I can't recall what was said, or who was crying, or how many praises Martin got about his academic achievements. My mind was focused on one thing and one thing only—that ugly Ellen woman.

Hell no, I couldn't forgive the woman who hurt my mother and took from me the only cold, remote, drunk-a-holic daddy I never had. Looking to the right of me where Mama sat and then to the left where Justine was, I could tell by the look on their faces that they were not paying attention to the preacher man either. And why? They were just like me. Wrapped up in their own bitterness and anger. White, hot anger. Anger that was about to explode into the biggest funeral scandal this side of the Mississippi.

"Excuse me…excuse me," Justine said standing up from her seat, interrupting the solemn occasion. "I have something I want to say about the deceased, Martin McBride."

"Excuse me, Ma'am. If you will wait until after the service, you will have ample opportunity to say your piece about the deceased," the minister said.

"Talking about the *piece*—talking about the *piece*," Justine said raising her voice. "This is the *piece*," she said pointing to Ellen, whipping her arms in front of her in a flamboyant stroke while pointing the accusing finger. "This is the piece right here who broke up my sister's happy home and left her a widow and her child an orphan. Stand up Ellen! Stand up and let the educated college folk see the woman who should have a big red scarlet "A" tattooed across her forehead right next to the mark of the beast—666."

"Hell's bells," Ellen screamed, jumping up out of her chair like a piece of popping corn, losing all composure. "I've had enough of the likes of y'all. Don't you and your white trash family talk about me like I'm the *damn* anti-Christ! All y'all ought to have the decency to cut your losses after all these years and be civil at Martin's funeral, for God's sake. If ya'll had been the type of people that he needed, he would never have left you in the first place. So just simmer down and shut your mouths or get the hell out of here and leave us in peace to mourn his passing."

And when she was finished with her sermonette she did that little nervous flapping thing with both of her hands. As if trembling fingers in front of her face was going to make her look like a lady after cussing a blue streak.

"Well, I never," Justine quipped as she tossed her pointed chin up in the air like an offended debutant. After the arrogant gesture, she motioned for us to get up out of our seats and follow her out the door.

And so we did. Mama and I got up from our seat, and marched right out of the funeral home in the middle of the service. Once we got to the car, Mama started in on Justine and began scolding her for embarrassing the stew out of her in public. And after that comment, things went from bad worse. I had to listen to them bicker about this, that and the other all the way back home.

The fight finally ended when Justine got out of the car, pranced over to her red Corvette, jumped in, and started to drive away. Just to tick Mama off, I waved goodbye to her and blew her a kiss as she drove off. That really added fuel to the fire. And because of my foolhardiness, we had to have one of those mama-daughter talks all the way home.

All things considered, it was a *rough day* that would have even *depressed the Devil*.

Chapter 22

What Goes Around, Comes Around

Time passed quickly the summer my father died. June, July and August went by like a Talladega racecar lickety-split into the sunset. We awoke, we wept, and we slept. And then, the next day, we got up and did it all over again. In between the small details of life, like fixing our morning coffee and going to get the mail, we rehearsed the good, the bad, and the ugly (meaning Ellen, of course) about that rough day at Father's funeral.

For an entire summer, I grieved myself sick. Martin's death had forced me to feel not only the present pain, but all of the pain I felt as a child when he abandoned me for his ugly, ugly mistress. The echoes of old feelings—loneliness and loss blurred together on the canvas of my heart.

With his passing, the ache of fatherlessness had returned with a vengeance. It was 1978 and I was beginning my young adulthood feeling sad, useless, and fragile even though I had managed to survive most of the *horrors* of that decade: the bell-bottomed pants, the turtle necked shirts, the flower-prints, the hideous sideburns, and last, but not least, the platform shoes and leisure suits.

Come September, Mama went on with her life making a career out of being a Mimi Makeup Consultant and I went off to the university. College just added more pressure to my anxious life. Being away from home for the first time in an unfamiliar environment and with such intense father hunger was a recipe for disaster. I promised myself that I would not allow my college years to be hijacked by a man. Mama had warned me about that too. "Maggie," she said, "don't you disappoint me and go out with every Tom, Dick, and Harry. You make sure they are good boys and, at the very least, believe in God. You don't want to live the life I lived with your father, do you?" Just hearing Mama say that infuriated me. How dare she even think that I would be stupid enough to end up like her?

Well, I *was* stupid enough to end up like her because, before the end of my first semester in college, I was chasing and trying to get the attention of every Tom, Dick and Harry. First, there was Two-Timin' Tom and then there was Demeaning Dick, followed by Heathen Harry. Every one of those guys was as messed up as a rat's nest in a whirlwind, cold and remote as the state of Alaska. The less interested they were in me the more I wanted them and the harder I performed to get them to like me.

It wasn't just Tom, Dick and Harry; it was any man who ignored me. If there were fifty men in a room—forty-nine emotionally healthy men and one jerk, I'd find the one cold, remote man, go and sit on his lap and then try to get his approval. Sane women flee from these types of characters, but me? I hung in there with a dogged tenacity, pursuing every one of them with my humiliating attempts to please.

Did the men like brunettes? I'd die my hair. Did they like needy women —I'd be a child. Did they like them strong? I'd be competent and aloof. Funny? I'd be a comedian. Smart? I'd study harder. Did they like big-busted women? I'd pad my bra. Skinny? I'd starve myself. Every date I had was like an audition. I never stopped to think about whether or not I liked them; it was always about whether or not they liked me.

Every October I fell in love and by February the boy had dumped me or I had dumped him and I was heartbroken again. As a stroke of grace, several decent, moral, emotionally available Mr. Rights did cross my path, but because I had been so damaged by my involvement with the Mr. Wrongs, I quickly drove them away.

As a result of all these horrible relationships and rejections, my self-worth was lower than ugly Ellen's baggy eyelids.

Did I fail to mention that Ellen needed plastic surgery?

Now, getting back to the story…in an effort to assuage my pain from these heartbreaks, I tried to comfort myself with everything college life in the seventies had to offer, alcohol being at the very top of my list. While growing up, I had been such a conforming church girl that I had not tasted even one sip of wine before I graduated from High School. Ok. I lie. I take that back—I took communion (with wine instead of grape juice) at an Episcopal church. But, once I was away from home and had no one to be accountable to, I threw caution to the wind, sobriety down the toilet, and was determined to find out why my father found the comfort of wine so appealing.

My drinking began my first semester. At first, I drank a couple of glasses of wine at one sitting, but in a matter of months, my consumption increased to four glasses, then five, then six. Before my first year of school was over, I had crossed that evil line and by anyone's standards—I was a lush—the girl who always brought her own bottle to campus parties so that she could cop a buzz before they could tap the keg.

During that season of my life, Mama would call me on the phone and beg me to curb the drinking—but back then, I was too hardheaded to listen. "Shugah," she implored, "You don't want to end up like your father all tanked-up on wine every night." But in spite of her heart-felt words, they fell on deaf ears. As far as I was concerned, I had to agree with my father. Being plastered seemed to make everything in the 70's better—lava lamps, disco, the Partridge Family, The Rocky Horror Picture Show—everything. At least for a short while. As the Good Book says, "There is pleasure in sin for a season." After the fleeting pleasures passed, I was left with the cold, hard, truth. There was an emptiness inside of me that could not be comforted. Even the best Cabernet Sauvignon couldn't fill the void in my heart.

And neither could a good-looking older man named Elliot Malone.

One day while bemoaning my latest breakup, I happened to stop by the coffee shop across the street from the University and there he sat—a sight for sore eyes. A charming rogue. A gorgeous man in his early thirties with stunning premature grey hair that accented his penetrating, azure blue eyes.

Come to find out, Elliot was a professor in the drama department. My attraction to Elliot was strong, immediate, and oh, so very familiar. I was drawn to him with a force that had the same feel and intensity as that of an innocent child wearing a little yellow polka-dotted dress and waiting by the window for Father to come home from work.

When I close my eyes, I can still see him sitting in the booth at the coffee shop reading an excerpt from William Shakespeare's *Much Ado About Nothing* through the lenses of his outdated horn-rimmed glasses—

> *Sigh no more, ladies, sigh no more,*
> *Men were deceivers ever,*
> *One foot in sea, and one on shore,*
> *To one thing constant never.*
> *Then sigh not so, but let them go,*
> *And be you blithe and bonny,*
> *Converting all your sounds of woe*
> *Into hey nonny nonny.*

There was no way for me to know at that time, that upon our first meeting the very passage I saw him reading was a foretelling of the way he conducted his relationships with women.

In a word—Elliot was a player. He could play women like a fine-tuned violin. I won't bore you with the details that would read like some trashy romance novel. Just let me cut to the chase and say that he was a betraying bastard and in less than nine months, he had my bleeding heart laid bare on the pavement. "Maggie, I think that you and I are part of a long tradition, Adam and Eve, Dante and Beatrice, Mom and Dad, and I want to build a lasting relationship with you." He uttered this flowery nonsense on our first date after strumming his guitar, reading poetry and feeding me strawberries with whipped cream.

In my stupid naiveté, I bit that line—hook line and sinker. I thought I was as good as married. What I did not know was that I was just one of many women he was seeing even though he was telling every last, gullible one of us that we were the one and only. While not quite the words of William Shakespeare, I came to find out that the smooth line he used to get me to fall for him was just that—a line from a play.

And so, once again, after reliving the heartbreaking theme of betrayal from my childhood, after the flush of infatuation, and after months of trying to get Elliot to love me—it was all over but the shouting. I woke up one day and realized that I was still holding out the hope that all the places in my heart that were still achy and empty would be made whole by this man. But, as we all know, this would never happen.

In time, I found out that he was just like my father—he would not, could not, cherish me.

Another relationship with a man that I had so desperately wanted had ended in despair. It was truly tragic and *Much Ado About Nothing.*

And so, after months of throwing myself at a man who obviously had nothing to give, I went to my apartment near campus, pulled out my journal and poured out my pain on paper by penning my own literary creation:

The Coffee Shop

I'll meet you at the coffee shop at dawn
Where the scent of cinnamon
Hangs in the air like an autumn morn
And the radio plays a sad love song
To mock our tired ritual
Eying a lonely moth beating its wings against the window pane
I ease into the staleness of the day
And hang on every word you say
Until the paper you hold becomes a fortress between us
And you remind me of my father–with that look
Without the wine and history books
Damn your academic eyes—the ones that rove and analyze
The ones that haven't realized
The heart of a woman runs deep inside
Passionless now, you reach for my hand
It feels like I'm your wife
And just as I curl my fingers around yours
You withdraw again
To fold the newspaper, not once, but twice
What am I doing here accepting crumbs from a sweet roll?
And twenty-two minutes of morning?
And this is all you give to me
A creamless cup of coffee
I watch you finish your second cup
The signal that our time is up
Humbled, I surrender to farewell

And you?
Too cold to tell that the child in me goes numb when we part.
Now you, and my father—have broken my heart
But for now, my life is this—killing time in a coffee shop
Feeling things I almost forgot
Before I met you
And in the bottom of my paper cup—there's a storm rising up
Tell the waitress I've had enough
Until I see you
Tomorrow
At the coffee shop

Once again, I had to let go of another remote, emotionally unavailable man. But not the memory of our last kiss. Even if the woman loses her man, she still deserves the bittersweet memory of a fiercely passionate kiss...

...the night was clear and yet black as velvet; dark as the crooked plans in the heart of Elliot. The stars shone brightly as the moon pulsed in the quiet sky—as if waiting for two ill-fated lovers to say their last good-bye. A flicker of light from a street lamp shone down upon us. The silence in our eyes became thick and ominous. It was time....it was time... he pulled his body close to mine. In a play of romance, he began to kiss me slowly on my forehead. He moved deliberately, gently guiding his lips to my eyelids...kissing...fluttering... caressing... it felt like a dance. And then to my feverish cheeks he went, where his lips lingered, pausing only to tease his hand down my arm, enfolding my waiting fingers. Unexpectedly, eagerly, he embraced my hand, holding it tenderly in his as if he really loved me again; such a cruel but charming lie. My heart was beating so wildly, I thought I might die. Then, raising my hand up to meet his warm mouth, he kissed my palm longingly, turning it about, followed by a delicate graze on the inside of my wrist. It delighted me so, leaving me breathless to resist. Looking deeply into his hungry eyes, I sensed that he was restless. And just as the madness of

passion seized him, just as he pressed his lips on top of mine,
convincing me that I needed him and was safe in that desire;
I came to my senses and realized that I had been tricked.
And that he was intoxicatingly, charmingly sick. And that I
was so very tired of his strange, conflicting passions that set
my soul on fire.

In that moment, I made a vow never to abandon myself to love, ever. Ever again.

For the first time in my life, I knew and understood my mama's pain; the pain of loving with no return. The pain of wanting someone who did not want me back.

A lesson learned the hard way.

The old saying is true: *What goes around comes around.*

Chapter 23

Nun at All

And so, dear reader, if you have recovered from that passionate description of the kiss, I'll continue with my story. I mean, it's not as if we got "necked" as they say in the South.

After being rejected by Elliot, I felt as if my whole world was coming to an end. So intense was my grief that not even a pound of chocolate, a bottle of wine and music by Neil Diamond could console me. And let me tell you that if Neil Diamond could not console me, I was in *bad* shape. I'd formed a crush on Neil the minute I laid eyes on him on TV. Many a night when I was just a smitten teen-aged girl, I would pray to God that somehow fate would be kind to me and by a quirk of circumstance I'd meet Mr. Diamond and we'd fall in love and he'd ask me to marry him. But alas, that fantasy never came true. I was stuck with the poignant reality of my relationships in Birmingham, Alabama and just Neil's voice on *the Hot August Night* album.

And so it went, instead of meeting and marrying my dream guy before I graduated from college in 1981, I rummaged through the lives of two other troubled men trying to find the one who could heal my lovesick soul. Neither relationship lasted very long. As crude old deacon Simmons back at The Flow used to say, "They all lasted about a long as a fart in a whirlwind."

And since being a lesbian didn't appeal to me (although it was beginning to be highly fashionable in the 80s, along with the curly, cockatiel-looking hair), I guessed I'd better consider another type of an alternative lifestyle—I could become a nun. As the old joke goes: "A nun's a woman who ain't had none and don't want none." But, the problem is, I'd already had some, so I would have to see if those Catholics were really strict about this, or if by some chance there was some wiggle room in the rules of nunnery.

Maybe in the process of finding out about life in the convent, the kind sisters could also help me straighten out my relationship with an angry God. Anyway, I thought it was worth a try. There was only one problem. In order to become a nun, I'd have to convert to Catholicism, and that would be a fate worse than death according to some members of my very Protestant family.

It was Mama's folks who would have pitched a fit. Not Mama. She was always fairly open-minded when it came to issues like politics, race and religion. Actually, she liked one Catholic in particular really well—JFK, as I have already mentioned. Mama was not the Catholic hater, it was her kinfolk. Being very prejudiced and judgmental, they put Catholics in the same category as whores and child molesters. They were so prejudiced against Roman Catholics, it was rumored, that one of my relatives remarked that he'd rather my father be a heathen than a Catholic because at least he would not be a hypocrite who blindly followed the Pope and believed in Mary.

Have you ever heard the old story about Catholics going out on Friday evening and getting drunk and screwing around after their fish supper, of course, and then showing up at confession on Sunday and getting to beg forgiveness, and then doing it all over again the following week? Well, that's about all I heard when that group of picky Protestants got together. They made bashing Catholics a pastime. Most of Mama's kin, being Baptists, they called what little they understood of the Catholic faith, "Greasy Grace"—the freedom to sin, again and again. So, if I were going to think about being a Catholic nun, I'd probably be disowned by most of the family. This being the case, I'd have to think long and hard about a conversion.

And so I did. I sat down on my sofa after supper one night and thought about it all of twenty whole minutes when I decided that there was no way in heck that I could Hail Mary and pray a rosary. I was a coward. I didn't have the courage I needed to go home to Rome. But, along the same line, I had another idea. As I recalled (when Clementine and I were in the throes of our addictions to the prayer line), I happened to see a woman in a habit at an Episcopal church. "If I could be an Episcopalian nun," I thought, "I wouldn't have to embrace the Pope, Mother Mary, or fish on Fridays. I could still be Protestant, stay in the good graces of my family, and hide out from everything that bothered me about men and the painful world I lived in."

And so, a few weeks before I graduated from college, I took a little field trip to a convent. An Episcopalian convent. Yes, dear folks, I had a little visit with the nuns—Sister Emily Mary, Sister Mary Emily and Sister Mary Mary. Those three women quickly educated me about the stark realities of living a life set part to God. Besides becoming an Episcopalian, I'd have to take vows of poverty, celibacy and obedience. Not exactly appealing to a young girl who had had already experienced some of the world's charms.

When the sisters asked me why I wanted to be a nun, I told them that I wanted to "escape from the hurts of life," which I thought was the reason any normal woman would do such a thing. In rebuttal, Sister Mary Emily informed me that the communal life was "not for escaping from anything and that whatever I was avoiding would find me speedily among all of the solitude and time for reflection." This was not what I wanted to hear.

"So what are you avoiding, Mary Margaret?" they asked. The sisters called me by my first and middle name, just like Mama did sometimes when I was a child. "I'm avoiding men," I said confidently. "Isn't that why ya'll are here? Even without make up and your hair scrunched up underneath that habit, or whatever you call it, I can tell that all of you are fairly decent-looking women. So, I just thought that any woman who would commit her life to being a nun must have done it because they are fed up with men or are just plain tired of wearing cosmetics. Am I right? I am right, aren't I?"

By the look on Sister Mary Mary's face, I knew that I had struck a nerve. She didn't hesitate one bit to tell me that I was "wrong as wrong could be" and that perhaps I could find God's will for my life by "going to therapy, not a nunnery." Well, with me being young and cocky, I didn't take her advice too kindly. In a heartbeat, the pride of youth overcame me and I marched right out of that convent with my hair tossed over my shoulder and my pocketbook swinging in the wind. I wasn't going to let Sister Mary Mary poop on my party. "I did not come here to have a woman of the cloth insinuate that I am touched in the head!" I said as I left.

When my anger subsided, I must admit, I was devastated. De-ves-ta-ted. It seemed like everywhere I turned I encountered rejection. Feeling so darn low, I wanted more than anything to get in a quiet place and have it out with God just like Job did, but we all know what happened to him: poverty, death of loved ones, boils all over his body. Gruesome—if I may say so myself.

I wished I could have been like my friend Clementine who (even though she was indeed a little touched in the head) was assured of God's love. She used to tell me to read the Psalms for comfort, but when I did, none of the good stuff settled in my spirit, just words like wrath, anger, displeasure, wicked, and disobedience leapt off the page. It was as if Satan himself were reading the Bible to me with some perverted twist—like the devil had masterminded an evil plan to get me to believe that God was not a good God, but rather a malevolent force that was out to get me. And I can't help but think that it started with that preacher who scared the Hell into me on the day I walked the aisle and became a church girl. His warped delivery of the gospel had set the course for my relationship with God for years to come. One day, I thought to myself, I'd look him up, and give him a piece of my mind. The piece that always had belonged to him because of the unforgiveness in my heart that bound us together.

Oh, how I wish that the nuns had let me into their little club. I would have hidden myself away in that tranquil place (and changed my name to Sister Maggie Maggie) until I could have emerged once and for all as either a God lover or as a godforsaken atheist who would be worse than my heathen father—a godforsaken agnostic. Somehow, the scale had to tip one way or the other or I was going to have a nervous breakdown. Even though, in hindsight, the nuns correctly discerned that I was running from my problems, and I didn't like it that they did—I, too, couldn't help but notice a pattern. There it was again: I had been rejected by religious folk.

Was I thick as molasses or was there somebody upstairs trying to tell me something?

Chapter 24

The Rapist

Just weeks after my day at the convent, I graduated from college. Mama was there at the graduation service to support me even though I had almost written her out of my life during my college years. Feeling tremendously guilty about the prospect of seeing her smiling and teary-eyed in the audience, I downed a few glasses of wine before the service and practically floated across the stage as the Dean handed me the diploma.

In spite of all of the drinking, dating and partying I did during those trying four years, I managed to earn a degree in journalism.

The journalism degree didn't happen by accident. My enthusiasm as a writer began in nineteen seventy-something when my mother found a pitiful country song I'd written on a tattered scrap of notebook paper and began praising me for it. Being the perfect Southern mama, she bragged on it as if it were the Gettysburg Address. "Shugah, this is simply precious," she said, holding the trite and clichéd masterpiece to her bosom.

"You using me-e to get to her-er and I know why-i
You can't come plain out and tell me because you're too shy-i…"

I was only ten when I wrote this song, but even now, I can feel the flush of embarrassment on my cheeks as I share this with you. Mama's inordinate praise gave me an overabundance of confidence. But this turned out to be a good thing. Mama's inordinate praise eventually paid off.

After graduation, Mama contacted her new best friend, Lolly Lacy, who was the editor in chief of a local magazine in Birmingham. With a few good references and an "in" because of Lolly, I landed a job. It wasn't the ideal job, but it was in a field that enabled me to use the skills I acquired with my journalism major. I was hired as a writer for a women's magazine that specialized in "how to" type articles. Although there was not an outlet in this position for creatively or originality, I gave it all I had and tried not to complain too much. Day after day, I showed up at my cubicle, sat down in front of my computer and cranked out drivel about how to make doughnuts out of biscuits, how to design your own greeting cards, and how to find the perfect gynecologist.

Upon one occasion, when one of my coworkers was recuperating from surgery, I got to take over her assignments as the self-help guru and write about things that might have actually meant something. Things like marriage, self-esteem and addiction. Having to do research on the dynamics of alcoholic families made me realize something that I didn't want to admit—I was every bit my parents' daughter. As I read the material in preparation for writing the articles, it became apparent that in spite of all the vows I made never to be like my parents, in too many ways, I was just like Careen and Martin. My father drank; I drank. My mother was codependent; I was codependent. History was indeed repeating itself and as the old saying goes, "the apple doesn't fall far from the tree." Convinced now that I needed help but not knowing exactly where to turn, I did what the nuns suggested and what most people in the eighties did when they were clueless—I went to see a therapist.

It seemed like almost everyone in the 80s had a therapist: church girls, heathen, everyone. I couldn't even go to the grocery store without hearing the woman in the line behind me talking to the woman in the line behind her about her latest therapy session. "Yeah, my therapist said I should sit down and process the whole thing. She said that my issues are what attracted me to Jim and that we would work through it in the next session. What does your therapist say about your relationships? Are they drunk-a-holic? Work-a-holic? Jerk-a-holic?"

Therapist—the rapist. If you look closely at the word, that's what it spells. TheRapist. It was just a cute joke when I first read about it in one of those articles at work, but then, I asked myself, "Why would someone make a joke and break up the word like that and insinuate rape?" And then, someone who had been in therapy for ten years told me: "Because in therapy, you are never finished. Your issues just go on and on and so do the bills."

The guy whose name was on my bill for my first and only therapy session was Dr. Henry Blair. Dr. Blair was trained in humanistic psychology with an emphasis in visualization, and as I came to find out, like most humanists—he didn't believe in God. And after talking with him for about fifteen minutes I knew exactly why he didn't believe in God—he thought he was God. I'm not lying when I say that the walls in his office were decorated floor to ceiling with every award and diploma he'd received since about age five.

Other than my immediate disdain for him, the thought of having my very own therapist made me feel important. Of course, there were a couple things that I would have to overlook including the fact that the entire relationship was contrived and I was paying big bucks for his attention. I also didn't like the fact that I'd have to pretend that the Doc was a cherished friend who cared deeply for me and not someone who was making a hundred dollars an hour and had been trained to say profound things like, "And how does that make you feel?" All things considered, I realized that the main reason I decided to enter the world of psychotherapy was that I would finally have someone to listen to me-me-me, because no one ever did. I was determined to make that arrogant shrink earn his money.

And so, the session began.

"Tell me about yourself, Megan. Tell me why you're here."

"Um… it's Maggie." Well, well, well, I thought to myself, you heard all about me on that psychosocial you just took me through for the past hour and you can't remember my name. You got Alzheimer's or what?

But I didn't say that. Of course, I didn't say that. No self-respecting church girl would say that. But what I did say was equally as sassy…

"Well…let's see… I'm here because…I'm here because…I've got… Leprocondria."

"Leprocondria?" He repeated it in all seriousness as if he really thought it might have been a diagnosis he failed to learn in grad school.

"You know, the fear of finding little Irish men holding pots of gold at the end of the rainbow."

He flashed a look in my direction, which told me he wasn't amused.

Then, as if he were seeing me for the first time, he leered lecherously in my direction, staring up and down. Eyes roving from head to toe. Up and down. Head to toe. Up and down. After he took his eyes off my legs, he repeated the question.

"Tell me, Maggie, why are you here? Tell me in one sentence why you're here. In just one sentence."

"Let me think…let me think," I said aloud. "Well, I guess I'm here, doctor, because my father didn't love me and my mother was obsessed with men and religion, and until this day I'm still scared of going to Hell, which makes me screwed in the head. How does that sound to you?"

The expensive doctor cleared his throat and repeated what I said, "Screwed in the head? You know, Maggie, the first thing you are going to have to work on—is your negative self-talk. What you put out there will come back to you. Now, I want you to take a deep breath and repeat after me: "I love the universe and the universe loves me.""

"You've got to be kidding," I thought to myself.

"Come on, say it with me—saaaay it…I love the universe and the universe loves me."

"Ah…no. Don't want to say it," I said.

"Come on, Maggie, don't be treatment resistant, say it with me…. saaaay it," he said. "I… love… the… un-i-verse… and… the… un-i-verse… loves… me."

By this time he was really getting on my nerves, so I did something those psychologists are always telling you that you should not do. I became aggressive… not assertive, Ag-gres-sive. "I can't say it, Dr. Blair," I yelled in his face.

"Why not?"

"Because…I don't love the frickin' universe and the frickin' universe doesn't love me. The universe is impersonal and, besides, if you had read my intake form you would have seen that I checked the box that read "Christian" for Christ's sake. Christians believe in a personal God, not the frickin' universe. Didn't you take world religions in college?"

And then he retorted, "If you believe in a personal God—then why doesn't your personal God help you with your personal problems?" And this he said all smug and self-assured. He continued, "If you believe in a personal God, then why are you sitting here in my office soliciting advice from a humanist?" And then smiling a sort of crooked, sexy smile, he looked at me and winked. "You got a little sass in you, huh? Sass—that's a good thing. I like a pretty woman with sass."

I had been in his office less than five minutes and he was flirting? Telling me that he liked me? I think I read that this is called "crossing a boundary." Whatever it is called, he sure was making me feel uncomfortable, but I played it cool as though I hadn't noticed the overture.

He interrupted my thoughts by saying: "Yes, Maggie, if you prefer not to love the universe that's your choice…your choice, Maggie. Not your mama's… not your father's, but yours. Do you get what I am saying? No one can take the power of choice away from you."

"Ok, I think I get it," I said—thinking to myself that this guy was a little weird, but I heard that they all are—psychologists, that is.

He tried another question.

"Well, if you can't be serious about why you are here, just tell me a little about yourself, Miss Maggie."

He was mocking my Southern accent—the one I recovered when I wanted to be accepted by Southern children as a child in Sunday school. I didn't like him already.

"I was an abused child, Doctor. My mama subjected me to olfactory torture. Stinky agony. When I was about nine or ten, I had to wake up most mornings to the smell of brains and eggs cooking in the cast iron skillet.

But before they were in that skillet, the cow brains were wrapped up in brown paper and tucked neatly in the deep freezer next to the pig's feet and chitins. What a smell! Mama would tell me to go get a steak or two out of the freezer and then I'd see the package labeled "brains and eggs" and know that it could tomorrow morning that I would awaken to that unforgettable aroma: That concoction from Hell."

"Maggie, let's get down to business. Dispense with the Southern antics. You made a good choice when you decided to empower yourself by coming to therapy. I don't want to waste your time and I don't want you to be nervous, I just want you to relax and lie down on this sofa and relax." He pointed to his black leather sofa, authoritatively, and motioned for me to lie down.

I started talking to myself in the privacy of my mind: "This happens only in the movies, right? Was he going to pull out a pendulum and put me in a trance?"

"Here," he said calmly, interrupting my thoughts. He put his hand on my shoulder and began to give me a massage. "Let's get you relaxed so that we can try an exercise," he said.

Right away, I felt unnerved, but I ignored my gut feeling and submitted to his leading. As a distraction, I tried a joke.

"So…is this a package deal? Therapy plus massage?"

"So, do you want it to be? You're a very attractive, sassy young woman. I'll bet you have a lot of men wanting to rub your shoulders?"

I laughed nervously and tried to pretend that I did not hear what I heard him say.

"So, Maggie, just lie back on the sofa and we will began the visualization exercise. On the first session, I have my clients visualize what they want their life to be like at the end of six months…your ideal life…go ahead… lie back, close your eyes and tell me what you see."

I did as he instructed. I lay back on the sofa and closed my eyes. I was trying my best to be transcendent, but gosh—I saw…nothing. Nothing but the insides of my eyelids and those strange white sparkly flashes of colors. But then, at first imperceptibly, I saw a pair of brown trousers out of the corner of my eye. "Oh, Holy Mother of God that we Protestants don't believe in," I thought to myself, "it was TheRapist coming too close to me." Denying his intentions, I opened my eyes and spontaneously uttered something at random spontaneously in an attempt to divert his attention…

"May I have some water?" I couldn't think of anything else to say to that would hold him at bay.

"Visualizing your perfect life makes you thirsty?" Dr. Blair smiled again and went over to the water cooler. He took a paper cup from the dispenser and filled it with water. He brought it over to where I was now sitting and tried to hand it to me. When he did, it slipped out of his hand and the water spilled all over the front of my white blouse and soaked my entire chest. In an instant, before I even knew what was happening, he grabbed a napkin from his desk and began to dab at my soaked bosoms!

"I'm so sorry," he said. "Let me help you with that."

"What are you doing, for God's sake?"

"Now, let's leave God out of this, Maggie. I'm a humanist. We like people, not God."

"I don't care who you like. Stop that!" I grabbed his hand and tried to get up off the couch, so I could grab my purse and leave. But before I could get my bearing and balance, he took his knee and pushed it against my privates. My petunia. My buttercup. Whatever those Southern mamas used to call it when I was little. Then, before I could wrap my mind around what was happening, before I could work up a good slap in the face, the jerk was on top of me.

Suddenly, I felt my adrenalin start to pump as a sick swirling sensation filled my head. And just as I was about to have a panic attack, I heard the cocky therapist's secretary page him over the intercom.

"Dr. Blair, your wife is on line two. Dr. Blair, line two. Your wife. She says it's an emergency."

When he heard that—you should have seen that sucker move. Just hearing his secretary mention his wife made him get off me faster than a coon dog after a hound. And me? Mama didn't raise no fool; I pulled my skirt down, grabbed my pocketbook and shot out of his office like a bat out of hell.

And this concluded my first and only therapy session.

CHAPTER 25

THE BEAUTY SHOP

AND SO ON THE DAY that I encountered "TheRapist" and wasted my hard-earned money, I went straightway from his office to a place where most Southern women feel safe and secure and loved—the beauty shop.

Every good Southern woman goes to get her hair and nails done when she is feeling blue and her spirits need a lift. When you grow up in the South, it is just what you do to keep yourself looking presentable, perk up your mood, and keep yourself from paying a therapist.

Mama and I had been going to the same beauty shop since I was knee high to a duck, which was called, interestingly enough, The Beauty Shop. We figured that the owner, Nona Ricky, was short on originality when she picked that name. But what she lacked in originality in selecting a name, she made up for in her personality and looks. Nona had a quick wit and a heart as big as her pink-tinted beehive hair-do. At forty-something, she still looked like she was in her thirties. Whether that was due to all the cold cream she piled on her face at night or to good genes, we didn't know for sure. Whatever the reasons, she was well preserved and welcomed each and every woman who darted in her door with a big, warm bubblegum lipstick smile.

There among the misty clouds of hairspray and the aroma of peroxide, her customers would sit under the dryers, eat moon pies, drink co-colas and sing old hymns like "Amazing Grace" and "How Great Thou Art" in chorus. Alma, the alto, was always a little flat on the harmonies and she stuck out like a sore thumb when she sang off-key, but we put up with her because no one was excluded from fellowship when you were at Nona's beauty shop.

On my way there, I stopped at the Quick Check and called Mama from a payphone.

"Mama," I said anxiously, "you have to meet me at Nona's just as soon as you can get there….I have just had one of the worst days of my life."

"But I just had my hair done three days ago," she responded. "What's wrong, Shugah?" (She still called me Shugah). "Tell your mama what's the matter."

"Not now, Mama…not over the phone…just come to The Beauty Shop and I will tell Nona to get her help to paint your nails….just come on!"

"Alright, Shugah…I'll be on over. I was going to go to my Codependency meeting, but you seem upset, bless your heart. I'll be over as soon as I can."

Would you believe it?—while I was still the same messed up woman, Mama had been getting some help for her problems at one of those 12 step groups for codependents. My very own mother had been smitten by the 12 Steppers. Mama was working her program, taking it "one day at a time" and "keeping it simple." She wasn't obsessed with men who needed fixing anymore and, most importantly, she wasn't trying to control me with her emotional neediness. Heck, she had even reconciled with her sister Justine. Because of the influence of that group and the new friends she met at the meetings she had learned to "put first things first," to "live and let live" and to "let go and let God." She also was able to memorize all of these ingeniously clever slogans, I just recited. Because of her newfound groupies, Mama was getting well and blossoming into a caring person who was comforting to be around. I think she had what the Steppers called "a spiritual awakening." And now, miracle of miracles—she was becoming like a best friend to me. A *best* friend.

Although I was genuinely glad that Mama was finally getting her rough edges smoothed out by her "Higher Power," being around her and witnessing her transformation only accentuated my misery. On that day at The Beauty Shop, I was ready to have a heart-to-heart talk with anyone in earshot who would listen just so that I could feel better. As the good

Lord would have it, it just so happened that I was in the right place at the right time. Just like the Bible says, *the steps of a good man are ordered by the Lord*.

Not that I was a good man, or a good woman, for that matter. I guess God gave me grace that day. I think it was Mama who once quoted another scripture to me that goes something like this: *It is the kindness of God that draws people to repentance*. God was being kind to me that day even though I did not deserve it. I had spent the best years of my life as a prodigal daughter, and in spite of it all, God was about to bless my socks off. Nona had hired a new shampoo girl and it was none other than the woman that I had met months before at the Purple Palace.

You must remember that I told you, dear reader, that our paths would cross again.

It was Essie.

As that awful preacher at the Baptist church used to say, "God has His ways." Surely, you remember her. The black lady I tripped over at the big purple church? Well, there she was as plain as day shampooing Alma's hair and humming a hymn. I would have recognized her anywhere with her radiant face and her voice as rich and soothing as the Holy Ghost Himself.

Her eyes twinkled like glitter when she saw me walk in the door.

"I knows your face. I knows that face. But I can't remember your name!" she exclaimed as she lifted her hands out of the suds and gestured towards me.

"Maggie," I said, and then she walked over to where I was standing and hugged my neck, leaving me wringing-wet with apple-scented shampoo. "The Purple Palace? Purple wall hangings. Purple curtains. Purple flower arrangements. The life-sized picture of the pastor on the wall. Remember?"

"Oh, Lord," she said. "I reckon I don't knows how I'd forget. And those pork and beans? You know, I didn't even have the heart to eat 'em after all the pastor put us through! Yesz, girl, I remember! How in the world has you been?"

It was right about that time when Mama walked in and we had ourselves a little reunion right there at The Beauty Shop. Essie told us about Nona hiring her a couple of days ago when she ran into her at Sears.

"I was just standing at the counter fillin' out an application when Nona leans into me and says, 'Why don't you just come and work for me? Can you shampoo hair?' and I say, 'I reckon any fool can shampoo a head of hair,' and well, the rest is history......cause here I am!"

There she was. An answer to a prayer I did not even pray. My feelings about God being an angry taskmaster were softening up a bit.

Mama and I settled in, plopping ourselves down on that old familiar chase lounge that Nona had bought at a yard sale when I was twelve. She handed us our Moon pies and co-colas, and I shared what was on my heart about my terrible day at TheRapist's office. But I did not stop at sharing that story but told many others about anything and everything that was bothering me. I laid my heart bare. Nona listened, and then put in her two cents' worth. Then, Essie listened and put in her two cents' worth. All the while, Nona was working her magic on me with my standard beauty regiment: a perm; a cut and style; a manicure. Long after Mama left to go back home and read her codependency literature, I was still there talking to Nona and Essie till late in the afternoon. Once, when Nona left the room and Essie was straightening up the salon and sweeping the floor, she turned to me and preached a little sermon:

"Maggie, I's only knowed you for just a few hours, but from everything I heard about your life and troubles, I'd say you need to be as worried about what you looks like on the inside as what you looks like on the outside. You come to The Beauty Shop to make your outsides beautiful...you needs to come to the Lord to make your insides beautiful. It seems to me you got a heart sore in need of healing."

I sat and listened.

She continued.

"Now, I'm not telling you—you have to....and I'm just suggestin' it....but I thinks that you could get help from some good, old-fashioned Bible teachin'. I walk with the Lord a long time now, girl, and Essie can teach you how God can heal a heart. Yes, I can. I can teach you about how God can heal a heart like yours. Just listenin' to you a while ago, I can say this....and I hope I don't offend...but you gots what the Bible calls a stony heart....Lord have mercy, girl, you gots so many resentments that it's a wonder you can even lay your head down on your pillow and sleep at night. You needs to deal with it now, girl. You needs to let the Lord in that heart of yours before it's too late."

And with that said, she bent down behind the counter and took something out of her purse.

It was a Bible. A worn and tattered Bible that looked like she had studied it so hard that the pages were worn potato chip thin and thoroughly marked up in blue ink and yellow magic marker where she had highlighted her favorite verses.

Essie thumbed through the pages quickly as if she knew exactly where she was going in that well-read book. Waiting in suspense, my heart skipped a beat when she turned that Bible around so that I could read where she was pointing. Her long tan finger ran down the page until it stopped on this scripture:

> *A new heart also will I give you, and a new spirit will I*
> *put within you: and I will take away the stony heart out*
> *of your flesh, and I will give you a heart of flesh.*
> *Ezekiel 36:26*

And then, she looked at me with penetrating eyes and said just one more thing: "If you will meet me here once a week on a Friday afternoon at four o'clock… when we close up shop, you and me can just go 'round back and sit on the porch and have us a little meeting. Is you ready for it?"

Well, I can't say that I was ready for it, but there I was looking all dolled up with my newly permed hair and fresh trim and all I could think about was that Essie was right. My insides needed to match my outsides as she so aptly put it.

"Yes," I said. "Yes, Miss Essie, I will meet you at four o'clock next Friday, here at The Beauty Shop."

And so I did.

CHAPTER 26

THE COME TO JESUS MEETING

AFTER OUR ENCOUNTER AT THE Beauty Shop, I went home and didn't sleep a wink that night. If I went to Essie's "come to Jesus meeting," I suppose it meant that I would have to "come back to Jesus." I did not know if I was entirely ready to return to Jesus. Especially not a "Southern Baptist Jesus." Perhaps I could return to Essie's Jesus. And if that were true, if I were to even consider returning to Essie's Jesus, then surely I would have to show up at her meeting like I promised.

In spite of my fears and misgivings, I made good on my promise and went to that meeting. Essie was right on time (showing up at four o'clock on the dot) and brought an armful of notebooks with her. Clearly, Essie was serious about her Biblical studies. Contained in those tattered notebooks was all of the inspirational material she'd written over the course of her lifetime. The lesson she taught had to do with the passage from Ezekiel that she showed me on the day we were reunited at The Beauty Shop:

> *A new heart also will I give you, and a new spirit will I*
> *put within you: and I will take away the stony heart out*
> *of your flesh, and I will give you a heart of flesh.*
> *Ezekiel 36:26*

"Look at that scripture carefully," Essie said. "The Lord say He will give you a new heart. That He will put a new spirit in you. That He will take away your stony heart and give you a heart of flesh instead. What you needs right now is open-heart surgery. You needs to let God open up that wounded heart of yours and take out the damage done by your bitterness, unforgiveness and rebellion."

"Rebellion?" I asked indignantly.

"Yes'm, to high heavens! Not only is you unforgiving and bitter, you is rebellious," Essie said, pointing her fleshy finger at my face. "You has been doing things your way, runnin' on self-will too long. You has been disrespectin' your heavenly Father by not acceptin' His Son, and the wonderful gift of salvation that He gave to us when He died upon that old, rugged cross. Look right here. Romans 5:8 say:

> *But God commendeth his love toward us, in that,*
> *while we were yet sinners, Christ died for us.*

Now, girl, that means that all the while you was runnin' from Him, neglectin' Him, being bitter and angry towards everything and everybody, Christ was still lovin' you and still woulda died for you if you was the only person left in the whole wide world. I tells you like it is. The price that the Lord paid to save your soul was a great big price. It wadn't no small thing. He paid a great big price. One day, girl, when I was layin' on my bed and just about to go to sleep, God showed me just how big a price He paid. I remember it just like yesterday. I was sayin' my prayers and askin' God to forgive me of my sins. And in a little while, I dozed off and had a dream so real-like, I will never forget it. I was walkin' with the Lord on that road to Calvary, just before he was 'bout to be crucified. I was walkin' right beside Him, watchin' Him suffer as he could hardly bear up underneath that big ol' heavy cross he was carryin' on His back. I was watchin' Him as he stumbled and fell. Watchin' Him as He looked kindly at Simon of Cyrene, who had done helped Him carry the cross. Then, after watchin' Him strugglin' from being so weak and beat up, I had to watch Him be crucified. My God, how He cried on out with pain as the nails was drove into His hands and feet. The blood was just a pourin' from Him as those cruel men raised up the cross. There He was. My Jesus. Hangin' on that old rugged cross. Dyin' out of love for you and me when we was goin' to hell in a handbasket. Dyin' so that you and me could be made right with God and have our sins forgiven and go and be with Him in Heaven when we leave this cruel world. As He was hangin' there on that tree, my Jesus was lookin' at me with eyes so tender and full of love that I thought that my heart would burst all to pieces. And then, right as I heard Him say, "Father, forgive them for they know not what they do," he turns His eyes in my direction, looks deeply and longingly into mine and with barely a whisper I hear him call my name…

Essie…Essie….Essie…"

I sat in silence by her side for what felt like an eternity. This deeply spiritual woman had touched me with her story in a way that was deep, profound and indescribable. There were no words. There were just no words to be said between us.

Essie finally broke the solemn silence: "Now, girl, I'm just talkin' to you like you was one of mine own children. Like you was my daughter. Now, girl, you need to be doing some serious thinkin'. You needs to realize a thing or two about yourself. You ain't so innocent in all this mess you been tellin' me about. You goes on almost two hours at The Beauty Shop talkin' about nothin' but the sins of everyone who has hurt you—your father, your boyfriends, your therapist, you even threw Ellen and your mama in that pile too. Don't you know that the bitterness and anger you is carryin' around is just as poisonous what they did to you?"

"I suppose," I said, sullenly.

"You is still mad at the Baptist preacher, you is still mad at your mother, you is still mad at your daddy and his butt-ugly mistress, you is mad at the whole wide world down deep inside."

"But, Essie," I protested, "Ellen took away my father and that minister was just plain evil. If you say you are a Christian—you shouldn't be like them. That minister Smith—he scared me to death with all of this hellfire-and-damnation preaching. I have been so afraid of God most of my life that just the thought of surrendering my will to His fills me with so much panic that I can't stand it. I have thought about it and thought about it and if I could find that preacher, I would have it out with him. I have tried several times to get his address, even the church he left does not know where he is. And with a name like Smith, he is hard to find. But someday, I'm going to find him."

Essie paused and said, "Well you know, girl, if God want you to find him, Hell or high water can't stop it. God will make a way. But in the meantime, you needs to get your attention off of Pastor Smith and put the attention where it belongs. On you. On you own sins and shortcomin's. It's you "standin' in the need of prayer," as that old song say. Not a person in this sinful world has ever loved like we should. We all falls short. I know that Essie is being hard on you but you young folk now days are just full of yourselves and full of pride. You needs to humble yourself under the hand of the Lord. I am tellin' you the truth as I speaks it. If you wants to get better, let God deal with that stony heart of yours. And don't you go makin' no eyes at me!"

Exasperated, I had rolled my eyes at her.

"You has been runnin' from God a long time just like that prodigal son in the Bible, except that you is a prodigal daughter. You needs to realize that God is for you, not against you. He don't want you to be walkin' around carryin' around all that poison. He wants you to trust Him. Can you hear Him callin' you back to Himself? Can you hear Him callin' *your* name?"

I needed to hear every bit of what she said, but I thought she would never finish. I was feeling so guilty and convicted that I wanted to get up, get out of there and drive away. At that moment, I felt like the most miserable person in the world. But before I could decide one way or the other, whether to go or stay, she reached over, and drew me close to her and wrapped her strong but tender arm around my shoulder. Then, as if she was my mama and I was her child, she put her hand on top of my head and pulled it over on her to rest on her bosoms. There in the twilight, on the back porch at The Beauty Shop, that strong and spiritual black woman was cuddling this twenty-something- year-old woman in her arms. As the day faded into evening, she sang a song to me that I remembered hearing when I first became a church girl. She sang it so soothingly that I was reluctant to move even a muscle…

Softly and tenderly, Jesus is calling—
Calling for you and for me;
See on the portals He's waiting and watching—
Watching for you and for me!
Come home! Come home!
Ye who are weary, come home!
Earnestly, tenderly, Jesus is calling,
Calling, O sinner, come home!
Earnestly, tenderly, Jesus is calling,
Calling, O sinner, come home!

CHAPTER 27

JOY TO THE WORLD

YEARS AFTER THE "COME TO JESUS" meeting with Essie, I still pondered the significance of that day. Every time I went to The Beauty Shop, she hummed that haunting hymn, "Softly and Tenderly," while she shampooed my hair.

After the day that we sat on the back porch at The Beauty Shop, there were no more intense talks with Essie. I guess she figured that if I could not make a commitment and serve *her Jesus,* there was nothing left to talk about. Essie was always loving and polite, but she never took me to that deep place in our conversations again. Instead, she humored me with her stories about her children and grandchildren and sent me home with a goodie bag full of homemade chocolate chip cookies and shortbread. On one hand, I appreciated her lack of evangelism, but on the other hand, I secretly wondered if she and God had just given up on me.

For seven years after that "come to Jesus meeting," I could not feel at peace within my heart no matter what I did. Drinking didn't do it for me anymore and neither did going out with men. I was still feeling troubled to the very depths of my soul. Pierced to the core. I found myself thinking about God more often, about my sins more often, and about the part I played in my misery. At age twenty-seven, I had worked hard at the magazine and acquired much of what the world admires and strives to own. I had a stunning eclectic apartment with a hot tub on the balcony, I drove a new car and I had substantial savings in the bank. As a young adult with so many worldly possessions, some would have said that I had arrived.

Even Mama was proud of me and never passed up a chance to invite me to the monthly women's luncheon she held in her home. Since I was still single, and still lonely, I attended many of the luncheons just to have something to do. Much to my surprise, the women at her gatherings were warm, loving and spiritual. Surrounded by all of this love and compassion, it was soon apparent that Mama was being transformed into a loving and compassionate person. Like the old saying goes, "birds of a feather, flock together." Mama had apparently found her flock and they were having a positive influence on her.

Much like strong, but loving, Essie, the Christian women who were befriending Mama were also steadfast in their faith and carried themselves with a dignity and grace that would make the best of women jealous. I knew beyond a shadow of a doubt that these ladies were the real deal— even if I was too prideful to admit it. I knew full well from reading the Bible that what I was witnessing in the lives of these women was this: they had *the favor of God* on their lives because they had made a decision to love and serve Him with their whole hearts.

I remembered the first Commandment:

> *And you shall love the Lord your God with all your heart,*
> *and with all your soul, and with all your mind, and with*
> *all your strength: this is the first commandment.*

That was my problem, I suspected. I had always loved God with part of my heart. But I had never given Him my *whole heart*. And I had never given Him my whole heart and was always running from Him because of fear. Tormenting fear.

The day that I came to that realization was in December of 1990. I remember the exact thing I was doing at that moment. I was sitting in my living room on my designer sofa sipping a cup of hot chocolate and half-heartedly listening to the Christian radio station. I was just a heartbeat away from changing the station to Classic Rock when this song played…

Don't run away from me.
Stay by my side.
We share a destiny, take my life.
You'll see I'm not like the others, the ones you've known.
They saw your weakness and left you all alone.
My love is stronger than the sunlight.
My love is brighter than the moon.
I want to be a gift to your life.
I'll never leave you—I'll never forsake you.

Through the storms, through the tears—
I promise I'll be here.
Through the trials you go through, I swear I'll stand with you.
You think you're running free.
Turn around. Turn around. Turn around.
You belong to me.

Don't turn your eyes from me.
Don't break my heart.
What stirs inside you is the love of God.
I'm standing here, bleeding here, pleading here with arms wide open.
Don't be afraid.
Trust what I've spoken
Turn around and stay.
Come rest your head on my shoulder.
Just lay your burdens down.
Your heart of stone could not be colder
But, I'll never leave you; I'll never forsake you.

Through the storms, through the tears—
I promise I'll be here.
Through the trials you go through, I swear I'll stand with you.
You think you're running free.
Turn around. Turn around. Turn around.
You belong to me.
My child, my child—you belong to me.

For God sakes! "What is happening to me?" I thought to myself in a panic. It was like I was being relentlessly pursued by a benevolent force even as I was running away from Him. Tears were beginning to well up in my eyes as I sensed that I was being wooed, sought after and yes, even chosen.

In an effort to not feel my feelings, I decided to get dressed, and go outside to get some air.

And so, on the evening of December 20th, I put on my jacket, left my apartment and began to walk. It felt good to be outside since I had been cooped up in the house for most of the day. Ever since I was a child, I loved the mild winter Christmas season in Birmingham—the hustle and bustle of shoppers, the cinnamon and evergreen smells, the decorations, and the carolers who just happened to be on the street corners singing as I strolled along. . .

Joy to the world, the Lord is come
Let earth receive her King
Let every heart, prepare Him room
And Heaven and nature sing!
And Heaven and nature sing!
And Heaven and nature sing!

At first, my thoughts were aimless, like sleepy waves being tossed to and fro in the ocean. Then random thoughts started swirling through my mind, like the taste of morning's coffee, or the testy interchange I had with the man at the service station when I last bought gas, or the Christmas gifts I needed to wrap or the bills I needed to pay.

Joy to the world, the Savior reigns!
Let men their songs employ;
While fields and floods, rocks, hills and plains
Repeat the sounding joy,
Repeat the sounding joy,
Repeat, repeat, the sounding joy.

But then, as always, when I was alone, my mind traveled back, back, back to my childhood where the pain that covered my heart like a thick blanket first began its veiling. I traveled back to the sermon about being a sinner in the hands of an angry God. Back to the little church girl who asked inappropriate questions in Sunday school. Back to the child who couldn't turn her cold father into a loving human being. Back to TheRapist. Whoever said, "Time heals all wounds" was a liar or else someone who didn't understand the human heart. Time had not healed my wounds, nor had any human being, come to think of it.

> *No more let sin or sorrow grow*
> *Or thorns infest the ground*
> *He comes to make His blessing flow*
> *Far as the curse is found!*
> *Far as the curse is found!*
> *Far as the curse is found!*

And then, as I kept walking and my mind was about to settle into a numb reverie, my thoughts awakened again to my own shortcomings—the bitterness, judgmental attitudes and lack of forgiveness that drove me to find comfort in men, sex, and drugs. On the tail end of that stream of thought, a new one began, a poignant one about Elliot. After all I'd been through in my life, after all I'd seen with Mama and her men, why in the world would I allow myself to fall in love with someone who would reject me just like my father did? My mind circled around and around this question without finding an answer.

> *He rules the world with truth and grace*
> *And makes the nations prove*
> *The glories of his righteousness*
> *And wonders of His love!*
> *And wonders of His love!*
> *And wonders of His love!*

Just as I had was spiraling down into the barrel of self-pity in spite of the caroler's message of hope, just as I felt that familiar depression trying to own me again, I happened to look up. When I did, my eyes caught an image of someone in the distance who was walking toward me. As I continued walking ahead and crossed the busy street, the image came closer into view. I now discerned that it was a man. A man in a pea coat. A man in a pea coat wearing a Santa hat and carrying a guitar case. The man who had captured my attention had stopped and was talking to a street person. Nearby on the bench where the outcast sat, there was a handwritten sign proclaiming, "Homeless, Will work for Food."

Scrutinizing the hungry man's face, it looked to me as if the storms of destruction had blown over his life while leaving any remnant of hope withered in the dust alongside the pigeons that had gathered around his feet. As both men came closer into view, I sensed the desperation of a lost soul in the outcast's eyes reaching out to the man in the pea coat like a needy child begging for mercy after a beating.

"Hey man, could you spare a quarter?" I heard him say.

The man in the pea coat, sat down his guitar, fumbled in his pockets, and found the coin. Placing the money in the palm of the beggar, the needy one grabbed a hold of his hand. The man tried to let go, but the street person was clinging tightly, weaving back and forth. Obviously under the influence, it looked like he was trying to steady himself. Wondering what was going to happen next, the man in the pea coat began to speak…

"It's OK, man. It's OK. I know that you don't know me, but I feel impressed to say something to you." And then, looking intently into the outcast's eyes, he continued, "and I want you to listen to me. Will you give me your undivided attention for just one moment?" His voice was at the same time calm and urgent.

And familiar. There was something about his inflections that struck a chord with me. Surely, I would have recognized someone as distinctive as he was with his silver hair and matching beard. He was an older man, but yet quite handsome.

"Well, I reckon. I ain't got anything better to do." The homeless man replied.

Appearing spellbound, the homeless man cocked his head to the side and looked at him expectantly.

The man in the pea coat spoke slowly as if talking to a child: "When I first saw you today, I felt that God wanted me to talk to you and give you some encouragement. I felt like He wanted me to tell you that He loves you and that He still has a wonderful plan for your life."

The outcast did not respond. There was only silence.

"Hey, buddy, did you hear what I said? What's your name?" the man in the pea coat asked.

There was a long pause before an answer came. "Henry."

"Well, Henry, I'll say it again. I want to give you a word of encouragement. And that word is that God loves you unconditionally, and has a good plan for your life. I'm Mark, by the way."

Appearing dejected and slump-shouldered, Henry let go of Mark's hand and bowed his head. "What kind of plan could God have for someone like me?" he grumbled. "Look at me, man. I'm a bum, a loser. Don't even know if I believe in God no more. So if the next thing you are going to tell me is that I'm going to Hell—you can't scare me with that. I'm already scared of going to Hell. Been terrified of going to Hell for years."

"And why are you scared of going to Hell?" Mark asked.

"Because I drink."

"And why do you drink?"

"Because I'm scared of going to Hell."

"You're in quite a predicament, aren't you?" Mark sighed.

"Hell, yeah."

The homeless person looked up at and Mark who didn't seem bothered by his disheveled appearance and his weatherworn face—all pocked and bulbous. Then, I saw Mark absently scratch his beard and then pull out a small Bible from his coat pocket. Fumbling to find what looked like a specific passage, he read it to Henry:

> *Look not upon the wine when it is red, when it giveth its*
> *color in the cup, when it moveth itself up aright. At the last,*
> *it biteth like a serpent, and stings like an adder.*

"You've been bitten by the serpent and stung by the adder, haven't you, sir?" Mark said pointedly. "Cunning, baffling and powerful it is, that old alcohol."

"How would you know?"

"How would I know?" he repeated compassionately. "Because I've been right where you are, my friend. Not in the same circumstances, perhaps, but I have been to the bottom."

"I guess it's plain as day that I'm at mine. You can smell me?"

Mark nodded. "Boone's Farm?"

"Yes, sir." He hung his head again, too accepting of humiliation.

"Hey, you aren't the only one who has been taken for a bad ride with addiction. I talk to grown men everyday who sit in my office and cry because of what their disease has done to them."

"In your office? Disease? Are you one of them psychologists?"

"No."

"Are you a doctor?"

"No."

"What the hell are you then?"

"A minister."

"A minister? Oh, crap! Like one of those shysters on TV who tell old ladies to send in their prescription drug money to their ministries so that they can buy big houses and expensive cars?"

"No, not like that. I can't say that I like TV ministers much either—but getting back to what we were talking about—you know what, Henry? In all my years of ministering to folks, I've discovered this truth—most people who struggle with addiction resort to drinking because they are trying to feel loved and to heal a broken heart."

"Ah, crap," Henry said again. "Why did you have to go and say that? I knowed it. My heart is slap broken."

I watched Henry touch his chest as the tears welled up in his tired eyes.

"Henry, can you name the person who first broke your heart?" Mark said.

"Yeah, that's an easy one. It was Papa. That man used to beat me so bad I looked like ground sausage. I started drinking when the beatings started. And kept drinking when the beatings ended. And then I married me a woman and she left me because I was drinking. So I kept on drinking. And because of that—shit. . . I lost my job, my house, my car…. I lost everything. So here I am with a heart that's busted all to pieces. What's a man to do but drink?"

Mark tried to put his hand on his shoulder again.

"You really don't need to be touching me," Henry said, and withdrew from the Mark as if trying to protect him from himself. "I'm all smelly."

"I've got news for you, sir," Mark said. "According to God, we're all smelly. It's the miserable condition of the human race. God doesn't care that you're smelly and neither do I. We are all guilty at the cross. Every stinking and smelly one of us."

I could tell by the look on his face that the street person was taking in Mark's words. Every one of them.

And so was I.

When Mark stopped speaking, there was a soft, sad silence. In that moment, I was beginning to get a little paranoid, suspicious that the two men knew that I had not been engrossed in feeding the pigeons as I pretended to be doing. I suspected they knew I had been eavesdropping on their conversation, hanging on their every word as if there were something in it for me.

But just as my attention had once again turned inward, I heard music. As I glanced in their direction again, Mark was sitting on the bench beside Henry strumming his guitar and singing…

> *Come, gracious spirit, heavenly dove,*
> *With light and comfort from above;*
> *Be thou our guardian, thou our guide;*
> *O'er every thought and step preside.*

Mark's voice trailed off as a smile flickered across Henry's face.

"My Mama used to sing that to me every Sunday on the way home from church. She's the only one who ever believed in me. Maybe God loves me after all."

Henry looked up at Mark with that question in his woeful eyes.

"Of course, God still loves you," Mark assured him. "Look right here," Mark said, turning in his Bible to Jeremiah 31:3:

> *… Yea, I have loved you with an everlasting love:*
> *therefore with lovingkindness have I drawn you.*

"I hope you're right," Henry replied, "but I wished I knew for sure, if I only …"

Suddenly interrupted by a winged intruder, he didn't finish his thought. Speechless now, Henry watched as one perfect snow white dove nestled down onto the bench next to him where he sat at on a bench at Five Points South.

One perfect white dove.

CHAPTER 28

KAIROS: GOD TIME

I KNOW WHAT YOU MUST be thinking. You're thinking that I'm exaggerating. That the incident with the dove really didn't happen after all. That somehow, I imagined it, or even worse, just made it up to make my story more believable.

But I promise you on a stack of Bibles that I didn't make it up. It was true. Among all of those nasty brown pigeons, a perfect, snow white dove swooped down beside Henry and landed at his feet as if providing some sort of sign that God was gentler and more loving than the preacher of my childhood had made him sound. I tell you, God as my witness, as sure as I live and breathe that that bird came and landed right next to Henry. I saw it with my own two eyes.

So, on that magnificent day, when I saw the dove, I knew that I couldn't let the moment pass without getting to know that distinguished man, the same man who was playing the guitar and singing unashamedly in broad daylight to the street person. Observing that simple occurrence in Five Points South moved me deeply, and filled my heart with something I had not felt in a long time, if ever—fresh hope.

Who was this man with his winsome ways and a heart of compassion? I didn't know, but I was going to find out. Not knowing what else to do, I jumped up from the bench where I was sitting and followed him as he headed down the street. Even if I made a fool of myself, I was determined to find out about the man who called himself Mark. And if I could get up the courage, I was going to introduce myself and tell him about the conversation I witnessed between him and the street person.

So, I walked—one block, two blocks and then three, right behind him. When all of a sudden, he surprised me by picking up his pace and running down a group of steps just off the street that led to what looked like a small tavern or neighborhood bar. As I paused at the top of the steps, he took notice of my presence, turned suddenly and said, "Do I know you?" And then he looked at me for a very long time before his eyes widened as if something had suddenly dawned on him.

"You are the young lady who was sitting on the bench next to us at Five Points."

"Yes. That's me. Guilty." I said, while shivering in the chilly cold.

"Guilty?"

"I was watching you, listening to you…well, to you and the street person."

After my admission, he looked up at me curiously and said in a somewhat fatherly way, "You need to come in and get warm. Come on in. I'll fix you a cup of coffee."

He opened the door to the building. I entered slowly and saw that it was not a bar but a coffee house.

"And you were listening to us because…." he said as he turned on the lights and hung up his coat.

"Because I needed to. . . wanted to. . . this isn't coming out right. . . you wouldn't understand."

"I might," his eyebrows raised. "Try me."

But before I could even get through a few sentences of polite conversation, I humiliated myself by bursting into tears. And not just a few dainty trickles down the sides of my cheeks —a torrent of red hot, messy tears. Some women still look pretty when they cry. But not me. When I cried, that day, I bet I looked almost as ugly as Ellen did.

"Is the coffee that bad?" The kind man said, looking at me with the utmost sympathy in his eyes and just a hint of smile on his face.

In that moment, I couldn't even answer him because I was so wrecked. It was as if the years of pain left me with no restraint at all; it just came gushing out of me. But in spite of feeling self-conscious, I didn't even try to stop myself. I just let it out. Acting like a blithering idiot, I told him about seeing the dove and how badly that I too, just like that homeless man, needed to feel like God still loved me in spite of all of my reluctance to love Him. And from there, I told the poor man more about my life than he probably wanted to know. I told him about my father and his remote, alcoholic tendencies. I told him about my mother and her descent into depression after the divorce. And I didn't stop with telling about my family pain, but I continued my story by touching on the ongoing spiritual struggle I was having to get to the place in my journey where I could surrender my life to God without fearing that he would be a cruel task master who would crush my spirit like so many of the religious folks I'd met. What I *didn't* tell him about was my horrible experience as a child at the Southern Baptist Church. I was thinking that since he was a minister that he wouldn't take too kindly to me talking bad about another preacher.

After an hour of me pouring out my heart to this kind man, he took my hand, looked me square in the eyes and said something that was so comforting to me; I still cry just thinking about it.

"I'm sorry that you're suffering. I truly am. It seems that most of your life you have been grieving some kind of loss."

Funny how someone telling you that they are sorry for your pain can make you feel less alone.

"Let me tell you something, sweetheart," he said as he sipped his coffee. "From what you have told me about your spiritual journey and all of the searching for true faith among a sea of toxic religious experiences that you and your mother have undertaken over the years, I would say that at some point, perhaps early on in your childhood, you were misled about the true nature of God and were spiritually wounded."

"Spiritually wounded?" I asked, feeling perplexed.

"Yes. Spiritually wounded," he replied. "Emotional wounds happen when someone damages you in your emotions. Physical wounds happen when someone hits you and hurts your body. Spiritual wounds happen when someone injures your spirit. Usually this occurs when authority figures in the church misrepresent the heart, the mind, and the ways of God and damage your spirit so that you have a hard time seeing God for who he really is. And from what you have told me you have a horrible time seeing God for who He really is as I once did."

"So, it wasn't all my father's and mother's fault?" I said jokingly.

"Probably not," he said, smiling. "Are your parents still living?"

"My father has passed. My mother lives about twenty minutes from here and is actually a fine person now."

"Good relationships with your father and mother?"

"Not with my father. But on the bright side, I have a steadily improving relationship with my mother."

"How so?" he asked.

"As many problems as I had with Mama during my younger years," I said, "lately, I've become painfully aware that I've been far too hard on her, and that she does have some sense after all. And—she is recovery. From codependency. She's going to those 12-step groups. Talking the talk and walking the walk and all that jazz. She has truly changed over the years. I went to visit her one ordinary day, looked across the table as we were drinking our coffee and realized that she is …better than me. My mama is better than me. She is a warm, caring, loving individual. She isn't clingy and getting on my last nerve. She isn't the troubled mother of my childhood anymore."

"I think that many of us had similar realizations about our mother's," he replied. "But getting back to our conversation about spiritual woundedness, I am convinced that if you will seriously contemplate when the pain first entered your spiritual life that you could identify the source of your wounding. And, yes, I know I am acting like your pastor right now. You will have to forgive me."

"Yes, you are acting like my pastor." And then, realizing that he was beginning to make me feel uncomfortable because he was getting too close to the heart of the matter (which was all of the negative experiences I'd had in churches beginning with my introduction to Southern Baptist Jesus), I quickly decided to change the subject.

"Now that I've just monopolized about an hour of your time by telling you more than you probably wanted to know about the life and times of Maggie McBride," I said, "I think that it would only be polite for me to ask you about yourself. What's your story?"

"My story? I'm Mark. Sixty-two. Ex-pastor. Current minister. A Widower. My wife, Linda died of cancer a couple years ago. To fill the void,

I run this coffee house. I do some counseling, run a few support groups and minister to the homeless when I am feeling particularly spiritual."

He chuckled when he said that.

"I don't like church very much but I do like God. How's that for a start?"

Mark scratched his beard and got up from his seat to pour himself another cup of coffee.

"You're a minister, but you don't like church," I said. "That's curious. If that's true then you are different from any minister I've ever met. Most ministers I've met seem to like having a church—a big building with a big congregation, almost as much as they like God. Or, that's the way it seemed. I remember one preacher that my Mama and I sat under when I was a child that was—can I say it? *Mean as Hell.* He preached the most terrifying sermons you've ever…."

"Not to be rude or insensitive," he interrupted while looking at his watch, "but I did not realize that it was getting so late. I am going to have to put on another pot of coffee, get out the sweet rolls and prepare for a meeting. A meeting that I think you would greatly benefit from. Would you consider staying?"

"What kind of meeting?" I asked.

"It's a meeting about healing. Healing the human spirit. We call it "Healing the Spiritual Wounded Woman." About five women attend. I think you'd like them and they would like you."

"Oh, boy," I sighed. "The last time I decided to get help it didn't turn out so well." I said, remembering TheRapist.

"It didn't?"

Not wanting to give him the gory details, I avoided the subject. "I'll stay," I said quickly. "I'll stay."

"You will?"

"Sure. I'm ready for something different."

And then smiling the warmest smile, he said, "I'm glad to hear you say that. So, it would seem that you, dear lady, are at the right place at the right time. The ancient Greeks had a word for that—Kairos."

"Kairos?" I asked.

"Kairos. The right or opportune moment."

CHAPTER 29

WHO ARE YOU?

EVEN NOW, THE MEMORIES OF the afternoon that I am going to tell you about are as vivid as a color picture show. The women—they looked normal enough. They were all dressed impeccably and each wore a winning smile. You couldn't tell from first impressions that they would have anything in common with this messed up church girl. Neat, clean, manicured, and so noticeably Southern, no one would have suspected that they had suffered through many dangers, toils and snares while engaging Churchianity.

But they had.

Come to find out, each woman had her own story about the wounds she had suffered in the church. After Mark opened the meeting with prayer, he introduced me to the women in the group.

"Maggie," he said, "I want you to meet five of my most favorite women: Lilly, Candy, Crystal, Lindie and Nellie. Ladies, meet Maggie. Maggie, meet the ladies."

They nodded. I smiled a smile that I was trying to keep to myself because with names like that—I half expected the entire Junior League to show up behind them.

Mark continued, "The way we usually work, Maggie, is that each week one woman gets a chance to share a story relating to emotional or spiritual wounding and we all give feedback and offer prayer. But, tonight we have something different planned. Tonight we are going to have a guest musician. I have invited a friend of mine, Caroline Carr, a singer and songwriter, to minister to us through her music. She should be here in just a few minutes. So why don't you ladies take a seat and chat among yourselves until she. . . ."

And just as he said that, a gorgeous dark–haired woman walked into the room looking like she owned the place. She had a guitar in one hand and a fancy pocketbook in the other. I eyed her up and down as most Southern women do when a new one comes into the group. Standing about five feet tall, she was a petite thing and looked stunning in her long white laced jacket and black high-heeled boots.

"Ladies," Mark said gesturing to the beautiful woman, "This is my friend, Caroline. Caroline is going to be sharing some of her original compositions with us tonight. I want you all to make yourselves comfortable and make her feel welcome."

The women motioned for me to come and sit beside them. I took a seat and settled myself. Mark turned down the lights. We waited eagerly for Caroline to sing for us.

Then, without any further introduction, she began to play her guitar with such passion and intensity that it seemed that the strings might fly off the instrument. The energy she put into the music was intense, mesmerizing. And when she sang, she sounded angelic with her haunting, but fragile and expressive voice. The song was about her struggle to come to a point of surrender to God.

Who You Are

Some say you're a passionate man full of tenderness and warmth
Some say you're an angry man whose fury is like a storm
To me you're just a phantom—a mystic from afar
How can I love you when I don't know who you are?
Once my love was like a child's love, innocent and pure
But pain has come and so have changes, now I can't be sure
Of giving my heart to you, of trusting when I'm blind
How can I love you when I don't know what I'll find?
Confusion reigns in me now, Oh who will save me from this death?
My life's a worn-out theme of doubt and fear and shame and bitterness
I am no prophet but I sense this madness coming to an end

If only you would give me faith to believe in
you again—to trust in you again?
So, come touch me now in those secret places where I love to hide
Tear down the walls that keep me from You, heal the pain inside
My heart is turning towards you. My mind is still at war.
I need to love You
Come show me who you are. . . .

I was speechless as she sang the last line. The power in her ministry of song left me wrecked and undone. Looking around the room, I realized that the other women were sitting as silently as I was, lost in the gripping, mysterious meanings the writer had expressed. I wished that I could have gotten inside their heads to know exactly what those women were feeling and thinking at that moment. I imagined that they, too, were probably pondering all the years they had spent in unrest, trying to figure out if God was a friend or a foe.

"And He did," she said, jarring me out of my musings. "And He did," she said, referring to the last line when she beckoned God to come to her and show her who He is.

Then, Caroline continued: "On the night I wrote this song, I sang it for the first time as a prayer and asked God to come into my life and make Himself known to me for who He really is. Astonishingly, it was like a dam broke in my heart. Torrents of pain came bursting out of me and, at the same time it did, the greatest sense of love and freedom I have ever known enveloped me."

Just minutes before she shared this song, I had been sitting there wondering if God were a friend or a foe." For the first time in a long time, I was thinking that maybe God wasn't a part of the nonsense I had witnessed and experienced growing up. Perhaps I had been confusing religiosity with a heartfelt relationship with God. But, I'm sure that you, dear reader, had that figured out long before I got to this point in the story. Well, of course, that is what I had been doing—confusing God with religion. But as Mama used to tell me—hindsight is twenty-twenty.

Caroline came. She sang. She played. She spoke. And then she left. And even though she had only been with us for a short while, it was like she took a little piece of my heart with her as she walked out that door.

"If everyone has gotten her coffee and doughnuts, I'd like for you to return to your seats so that we can go ahead and start," Mark said, interrupting my envious thoughts. "We are going to review the basics since Maggie is new to us, so get comfortable so that we can begin."

Spiritual Woundedness. Let's define it: Having poisonous encounters with people or organizations that misrepresent the mind, the heart and the ways of God in a way that damages the person's ability to have an intimate, healthy and life-affirming relationship with his or her creator. Look around you, ladies. The reason all of you are here is because you have gotten connected with an individual, a church, a pastor, or a congregation that was cultish and abusive to your spirit, which is the part of you that should be able to intimately connect with God. At some point in your lives, you internalized an angry, punitive, distant or uncaring God whom you could not trust. If you had been presented with an accurate picture of whom God is, then you would instinctively want to draw closer to this power who is far greater than you, who is a loving Father and who always has your best interests at heart.

Loving Father? I never thought of God like that. A dictator? The Mafia? Yes. But a loving Father?

And many times the concepts of God we have internalized come from our own relationships with our earthly fathers.

When he said that, it was as if a light came on in my head. I guess I thought that God was like my earthly father— a cold, remote, distance, emotionally unavailable, punitive male parent. Are there any other adjectives that I've left out?

Many women think their Father in Heaven must be just like their earthly father. If you had a loving father, then you will have an easier time trusting in God the Father. But if you had an abusive father, then you will have a very hard time trusting your Heavenly Father, unless you allow God to heal you.

"That's me," I thought, as his words became revelation in my heart.

The first thing you need to do is to ask God to remove all false images of Himself from your heart and mind and to give you the grace to see Him as He really is...

It was that easy? Is he kidding? After all the agony I'd been through, you're telling me it could be healed with a simple prayer like that. It sounded too good to be true. There must be a catch, I thought. What else do I have to do? Fast? Pray in Tongues? Give Mark a tithe?

There are no hoops to jump through, no long prayers to be prayed, no fasting, no money to give, no penance to perform, no sacrifices to make. Just pray that simple prayer with sincerity of heart and sit back, relax and watch God work. And I promise you, yielding to the Spirit will heal your life. He healed mine when I was a mess in my younger years. I, too, had internalized a false concept of God as being angry and distant and vindictive and punitive. But instead of suffering innocently, as you dear ladies, I was on the other side of the fence. Not a victim, but an abuser. An arrogant, full of myself, angry, deceived young man who beat people over the head with Scripture and admonished them to turn or burn.

Then the women turned to me and said, "Here it comes, Maggie, you gotta watch this…he is sooo funny when he does this…"

With his natural charisma, Mark flipped into what appeared to be the role of an uptight, sour fundamentalist preacher who was getting ready to deliver a sermon. Intentionally being dramatic, he was camping it up by his flamboyant mannerisms. The way he was using his voice by taking it down a pitch or two and making it tremble made it sound remarkably like the preacher did back at the church Mama and I attended when I was young—Grace and Truth Baptist.

"Yes, ladies, I used to stand behind the podium every Sunday and terrorize my poor congregation with awful things like this quote from one of Jonathan Edward's sermons:He is not only able to cast wicked men into Hell, but He can most easily do it... The old serpent is grasping for them; Hell opens its mouth wide to receive them; and, if God should permit it, they would hastily be swallowed up and lost...."

I tell you the truth—I belly laughed for a few minutes, but then something strange began to happen to me on the inside. While hearing Mark dramatize this familiar tale of horror it triggered in me the memory of the experience I had as a child, the day I bolted out of the pew, ran down the aisle, and became a church girl. There in that coffee shop in the presence of Mark and the women, my poor heart started beating like a humming bird's. Ninety miles an hour. I thought it was going to jump out of my chest. I felt dizzy. Sick to my stomach. Sweat was popping out on my forehead.

Meanwhile, Mark continued while gesturing wildly with his arms as if directing traffic...

There is not a created thing not manifest before Him, but all things are naked and open to His eyes—with whom is our reckoning. Come as the choir sings the fourth verse again. Come, with every head bowed and every eye closed. Come, with no one looking around at their neighbor. Come now. And no peeking!

The women, who remained oblivious to my panic attack, began to laugh heartily. They were cackling like chickens and poking each other in the ribs as if they were sharing an intimate family joke. But, not me. I could not share in their laughter. I was now in another world, in the midst of one of those "Aha" moments, as it became crystal clear why Mark seemed so familiar to me. I had finally figured it out. He was familiar to me because, oh my God, he was that "MEAN AS HELL" PREACHER FROM MY CHILDHOOD AT THE BAPTIST CHURCH WHO SCARES THE LIVING DAYLIGHTS OUT OF ME and who has caused immeasurable spiritual anguish throughout my life. The realization came on me without mercy and like an epiphany in a made-for TV drama. If someone had had a video camera, my sudden display of emotion would have been good entertainment for years to come.

As the truth hit home, anger was coursing through my body from the tip of my toes to the top of my head. I was tingling, trembling, shuddering. And God as my witness, it took every bit of restraint I could muster not to go over to where the man was carrying on like an actor in a bad B-grade movie and ring his ever-loving neck. All my pent-up anger was ready to come out of me and explode like a lid flying off a pressure cooker.

So, forgetting all about the Ten Commandments, and number six in particular where we are commanded that we shall not murder, I just went with it.

Abandoning all of my good sense, I leapt up out of my chair, pointed my shaming finger in his face and howled at the top of my lungs: "You are the one! You are no nice and kind spiritual man who ministers to the homeless. You couldn't be—you hypocrite! What you did was so sorry; the devil wouldn't even want you. You may be fooling these women, but you are not fooling me. You are the sorry man who caused me nothing but spiritual pain! You are the "mean as hell" preacher who has been at the top of my shit list since I was a child. Well, well, well, if it isn't the almighty Pastor Smith from Grace and Truth Baptist. It's all coming back to me now. Clear as a bell. And I remember your wife Linda (God rest her soul) who, for your information, ridiculed me when I asked about Thelma Lou Cratchett, that guilt-ridden woman who rededicated her life every blessed Sunday. I'll tell you what I'd like to do to you when God's not looking. I'd like to knock you to Hell and back and then some. If I were your mama, I'd jerk a knot in your tail!"

And then without even hesitating, I did the unspeakable. I lunged in his direction, doubled up my fist and hit him with my best shot.

This five-foot-five, one hundred and twenty pound woman punched the man square in the face. Yes, folks. I hit a minister of the Gospel. A reverend. A preacher. A man of God. Any brownie points I'd been earning with Divinity just went down the toilet with that one act of craziness. And then, seeing that I was obviously not in my right mind, the women rushed over to where I was standing, grabbed my wicked fist and walked me straightway into the ladies' restroom.

"I think it's time you calmed down, honey, and get a grip," they said. "Let's get a cold compress on your forehead. You look like you could pass out at any moment here."

Well, I didn't resist them and, so, there we were. The women and I—huddled together like a can of sardines in that small ladies' room. And since there wasn't anywhere else to sit but on the toilet, that's where I plopped myself down while five kind women stood in a circle around me trying their best to make sense of what I was telling them about my history with Mark and why I had gotten so ill with him.

As I sat there on the toilet, trying to get my wits about me, I realized something: In spite of the horrible circumstances, in spite of my abominable behavior in their place of ministry, I'd never felt so much love and acceptance in my life. After years of feeling so unloved and unwanted in the family of God, I was surrounded by help and compassion. Lily Beth was patting me on the back. Candy was rubbing my forehead with the moistened paper towel. Crystal was holding my hands and Nellie, well; she was standing over in the corner saying a prayer under her breath. These precious women whom I had just met were showing me God's love as they accepted me in my distress.

"Honey, I don't know what you were so mad about, but whatever Mark did back then, you gotta realize that he's a different person now. And I'm sure that if you went back in there he would apologize to you," Lily Beth said in her calm, syrupy Southern drawl.

"Yes, precious, I know he would," Candy whispered while wiping the sweat from my fevered brow. "Ever since I've known him, he's been willing to say he's sorry when he's been wrong."

"So when did this happen?" I asked sarcastically.

"Well," Lindie said, "he's been like that as long as I've known him."

"Look," Crystal remarked. "It's no secret that Mark used to be much different in the past than he is now. It's part of his testimony, how he allowed God to work in his life to change him from being a self-righteous Pharisee to a kind, compassionate man. I'm sure that when you calm down, he will be glad to sit down and talk with you about this whole thing. You need to sit down with him and have a heart-to-heart."

"I agree," Nellie chimed in, "you two need to have a little heart-to-heart talk and put this behind you. Any fool can see that this is no accident—meeting up with him after all these years. You'd better not just chalk it up to a coincidence. You'd better pay attention and let God work in this situation. This could be the divine appointment you've needed all these years. Don't miss your appointment, Maggie," she said. "Now, you just get yourself on home, and think about what we've said during this little toilet moment, you hear?"

"I will," I promised. "I will."

And even though the women were as sweet as pie, they were not fully aware of what had just happened to me.

In all honesty, I think I had a breakdown that day.

Thank God.

CHAPTER 30

HEART TO HEART

AFTER THAT CURIOUS TOILET MOMENT with the gals from the Spiritually Wounded Woman group, I decided to leave the place before I made matters worse. Nellie was right. I needed to go home, calm down and collect my swirling thoughts.

So I did. I tucked my tail between my legs and headed home to call it a day, for it was getting late, around seven o'clock or so, and I had made a fool of myself. I needed to go home, seclude myself and lick my wounds. Recover from the trauma of it all.

By the time I returned to my apartment, it was nighttime. The day that had been bathed in light from the sun was now in shadow, sullen and dark. The memory of the carolers on the streets of inner-city Birmingham faded as their song to "Joy to the World" lost its life in the sadness of my worried mind.

While sitting on my sofa all snuggled up in a new throw that Aunt Justine had purchased for me at a boutique in Mountain Brook, the realization of what had some to pass concerning by reunion with Mark Smith hit me like a ton of bricks. Essie was right. God had made a way for me to get things right with that man.

Just the thought of having a heart-to-heart talk with the person who had caused me so much spiritual pain made me feel sick to death. Anxious. It was as if, all of a sudden, I could no longer see the kind man who was ministering to the homeless person, Henry, on the street—just his tense, angry, former self. Blinded by past bitterness, I struggled to find the right words to say in a "heart to heart" talk. I thought about telling him so many things, mostly out of anger.

The problem was—I had already made the mistake of hitting the man—and in the face, no less. With that offense, I really could not imagine that Mark would have been open to anything else that I had to say. Do you blame me?

Coming to no good conclusion on the matter, I simply gave up.

I gave up.

I decided to call it a day, put on my nightgown, tuck myself into bed and give the whole matter a rest. Give the whole world a rest. But just as I had that thought—there came a knock at my door.

Nervous as all get-out, I looked out the window. Through the sheers, I could see a man, whose features were being illuminated by the glow of the porch light, shivering in the cold. Gray hair. Scruffy beard. Blue pea coat. He was leaning against the banister holding a large sack.

It was Mark.

I didn't think I was ready for this. Not by a long shot. But as much as I wanted to hide in the back bedroom to make of this all go away, I knew I couldn't. Even as a church girl who had spent most of her life keeping God at arm's length, I knew enough to know that God's name was written all over this.

Our paths had not crossed by coincidence. It was a divine appointment.

I opened the door. "Well, don't just stand there in the cold," I told him. "Come on in. Maybe we ought to have one of those heart-to-heart talks like the women in your group suggested. How's your face?"

"It's the same old face I've always had with the addition of this memorable black eye," he said humorously.

Feeling totally humiliated and not nearly as angry as I was when I hit him, I made a lame attempt at an apology. "I've never done anything like that in my life. There's no excuse for my behavior. None whatsoever, no matter what. So, come on in out of the cold. I promise, cross my heart, I'll keep my hands to myself."

"That would be a good promise, Maggie," he said with a smile and a hint of sarcasm in his voice. "But I can't stay. I just dropped by to tell you that I am also very sorry and to give you these."

So there he was, the spiritual terrorist of my childhood with his outstretched arms handing me a sack filled with gifts. I took hold of the bag with my trembling hands and thanked him as graciously as I could. With a grin on his kind face he said, "Call me if you want to talk...here's my number." Then, putting the curled up piece of paper in my hand, he turned quickly, walked down the sidewalk, got into his car and drove away.

I watched him as he disappeared; feeling devastated in heart, as if haunted about losing a lost loved one. When I looked at his phone number, what a horrible emotion seized my soul—nervousness like I felt when I heard the sound of thunder as a child. And I...I was left alone in my apartment with many unanswered questions. He was certainly mysterious, this apparently changed man. I was extremely curious to know how he got from point A to point B—how he changed from being a self-righteous Pharisee into a decent human being. Eagerly, I looked inside the sack, and not only was there a bouquet of flowers, a box of chocolates, but there also was a letter with my name on it. Full of anticipation, I scurried to the kitchen, put the flowers in a vase, the chocolates in the fridge and then returned to the living room. Making myself comfortable on the sofa, I opened the envelope and began to read:

> *Dear Maggie,*
>
> *You have been on my heart ever since you walked out the door earlier in the day. I am sure that is was not by accident that our paths crossed. When God reconnects those who have been estranged for so many years, I have learned to pay attention. I write because I owe you an apology. It is my prayer that you will get in a quiet place and reflect upon what I have to say.*
>
> *First of all, I want to apologize for not remembering you or your mother. Even after I heard most of your story, I did not piece things together.*
>
> *Having said that, I want to be as honest with you as I possibly*

can be and explain from a spiritual perspective why I was such an obnoxious disgrace for a preacher and how grace lifted me out of that horrible pit of self-righteousness, legalism and fear. Hopefully, this will help you on your road to healing.

You see, Maggie, you and I have something in common and that is—spiritual woundedness. Like I said in class, instead of me being a victim of spiritual woundedness, I was a perpetrator. When I was pastor of Grace and Truth, I was one of those men who were out to build their own little kingdom at the expense of others. To be honest, during that season of my life I was a man given to anger, pride, and the need to wield control. Like you, I had a false concept of God as being mean and punitive, and I lived and preached that belief until I suffered a personal tragedy.

About the tenth year into my pastorate, my wife, Linda, was diagnosed with breast cancer. Instead of receiving the compassion and the support I needed to get through this difficult trial, the church members offered nothing but judgment and condemnation. Apparently, I had done such a good job of teaching a graceless, Christianity that as Linda's health worsened and she passed away, I reaped what I had sown. Following her funeral, certain members of the congregation told me that it was my fault that Linda had not recovered because I had not prayed enough, had not fasted enough and did not have enough faith, or else she would have been healed.

This event was my wake-up call. When I was at my lowest and should have been comforted, I was battered—spiritually battered. As cruel as it was, I knew deep down that I deserved the treatment and the accusations because I had been training up my congregation up to be hard and cold and legalistic since the day I became their pastor. It was like a slap in the face, but one that I needed and deserved.

And so, after the funeral, I went home and spent some time alone with God. I stayed in the house for three days, got down on my knees, and prayed for God to change me from the inside out. Gratefully, He heard my pleas and answered my prayers. He cleansed me from all of the false concepts I had of Him and replaced them with the truth about who He really is. He admonished me to forgive everyone who had hurt me and also to stop judging them.

After that discovery, I felt like my walk with the Lord could really begin in earnest. I am certainly far from spiritual perfection, but most people who know me now say that I have come a long way in learning to accept the grace of God and to share this wonderful gift with others. So, my best advice to you is to draw near to God because He tells us that if we draw near to Him that He will draw near to us. Lift up in prayer everyone you have judged and not forgiven. Then, release them from your judgment and unforgivness. Then, ask for God's blessings to be upon them. This healing act of forgiving others frees you from anger and resentment and leads to a richer and happier spiritual life.

Can you do this, Maggie? Do you want to free yourself?

When you are willing to let go of judging—grace and more grace will pour into your life as it poured into mine. It is miraculous what a heartfelt prayer and the power of God can do.

In closing, I just want you to recall something you learned in Sunday school a long time ago. Do you remember the words to that little song you sang, "Jesus loves me, this I know, for the Bible tells me so"? Well, don't become so grown-up that you can't grasp the heart of the gospel in John 3:16: For God so loved the world that He gave His only begotten Son that whosoever believes in Him shall not perish, but have everlasting life. God so loved the world, Maggie. And Jesus loves you. This I know.

Yes, God is love. He loves spiritually-abusive pastors, money-hungry evangelists, self-righteous Christians, toxic church girls, remote, alcoholic fathers, codependent mothers, and even bitter, judgmental daughters. He loves us all and knows that we can learn to love and serve Him even out of our brokenness.

And last, but not least, you have to believe that God is not mad at you. He poured every last bit of His anger out on the cross. The death of Christ brought peace between God and us. We were reconciled. Brought near. When Jesus hung on the cross and said that it was finished—He meant just what he said. It was finished. The striving. The works. The shame. The rejection. The anger. The loneliness. The fear. All of this can be healed because He overcame it all.

Now, take a little fatherly advice from an old man: You need to stop thinking that you are a disappointment to God and earnestly focus on His goodness, His love and His mercy.

As for the trouble in your life, surrender it all up to Him and do as I said in class—sit back, relax and watch God work.

By His grace,+
Mark Smith

CHAPTER 31

FIERY LOVE

AFTER READING THAT LETTER, I was dumbstruck. Mark really knew how to diffuse a girl's anger by bringing gifts as endearing as a bouquet of flowers, a box of chocolates and a heartfelt letter. How could I stay angry with a man who made such a charming apology with his chivalrous display of manners? How could I shun a man who gave me such valuable insight into my spiritual struggles? How could I resist chocolate?

I couldn't.

It was disconcerting, to say the least, remembering Mark as the man who was on my shit list for years and then meeting him years down the road as a changed man with a tender, passionate heart. He truly wasn't the same person. His transformation was almost unbelievable. I was stunned. From the words in his letter, I felt in my heart that he really had been converted. The man who used to be the arrogant, know-it-all, spiritual abuser was now a man of humility and compassion.

But the woman who had just read his letter was full of pride.

That would be me.

If not only for his sake, but also for mine, I knew that this chapter in my life had to come to a close. I had to forgive him and let it all go. I had to get him off my *shit list* and get on with my life. And I definitely, definitely, had to give up cursing because as every Southern woman knows—it's just not ladylike to curse.

As I sat there on the sofa, I thought about everything that I had just read and everything that I had heard Mark teach in class. And then I had another thought: at some point in my life, I need to *quit thinking*. Even with my best efforts, thinking had gotten me nowhere. All of the events that had transpired over the past two days had made it plain to me that I was wandering aimlessly in the valley of indecision whether I wanted to be or not. It was time to do something about my spiritual life...

"TODAY, IF YOU HEAR HIS VOICE, DO NOT HARDEN YOUR HEART."

Those words rose up from the depths of my spirit with a force of their own. Apparently, my Sunday school teachers had taught me more scripture than I had given them credit. It was as if the Spirit of God impressed upon me the urgency to draw near to Him.

And so, responding to the call of the Spirit, while sitting all alone in my living room, I made a decision to surrender. Or rather, God gave me the grace to do so. I was tired of being angry, tired of being worried, tired of being scared and most of all, tired of being lonely.

Feeling all queasy inside, I humbled myself, bowed my head, and prayed just like Mark had recommended. I uttered no thee's, no thou's, and no other fancy words from the ever popular King James translation of the Bible. Yes, I ditched religion that night and prayed a simple, heartfelt prayer.

> *Dear God, please, help me.*
> *Please open up my eyes so that I can see you for who you really are.*
> *Take all of my bitterness and unforgiveness.*
> *Help me to release all of the people I have judged from my judgment.*
> *Come into my life and heal my lonely, broken heart.*
> *In Jesus' name I pray.*
> *Amen.*

That was it. That was the prayer. Nothing flashy or complicated. Nothing religious sounding. Just me talking to God. And yes, I'd prayed many times before, but this felt like the very first time for some reason. Maybe it was the first time I was really sincere.

Who but *God* really knows the heart of a jaded church girl?

And after I prayed, I sat back, relaxed and *expected* God to work. Being a realist, I didn't really expect Him to work *that night* but sometime in the days to come. After all—I was tired. Having had an emotionally-packed two days, I really wanted to crawl into bed, eat some of those chocolates Mark gave to me and go to sleep. That's what I wanted to do, but as you will see, God had another plan in mind.

About an hour or so later while I was still sitting on the sofa and going back and forth between a half-asleep and half-awake state of mind, I heard a sound. Not an audible sound, but something in my heart.

It's not about what you can do, it's about Me.
With Me, all things are possible.

It was the still small voice. Soft. Clear. Unmistakable.

I sensed in my spirit what God was trying to tell me and it was good news—that He didn't need or want me to do anything. All I had to do was to . . . "sit back, relax and watch Him work." Just like Mark had said. What a relief.

Resisting the urge to get up and get busy just to break the uncomfortable solitude of my surroundings, I made myself sit still on the couch and concentrate on quieting my mind again. Then, I took a few deep breaths, laid my head back and closed my eyes. The minutes passed by slowly, but soon I was drifting…drifting. . . drifting back to that painful time in my childhood that I had tried so hard to forget…

I was five years old, waiting by the window for my father to come home from work. I could see myself clearly in my mind's eye, sitting on the couch with my legs crossed, wearing my frilly, yellow polka-dotted dress, peeking anxiously out the window from behind the curtains. Full of hope and expectation, I just knew that this was the day that things would change and I would capture my Father's attention. Earlier in the day, alone in my room when no one was looking, I stood in front of the mirror and rehearsed what I was going to say when he arrived: "Roses are red, violets are blue, I love you the most-est, do you love me too?" And after reciting that little poem, I would look up at him with adoring eyes and smile an irresistible smile that Southern children

*perfect. And then, unlike all of the times before, when I had
been shunned and ignored, he would give me the response
I wanted, pay me some attention, and say exactly what I
wanted him to say: "Of course, I love you, Maggie, —you're
my baby." I was sure this time that he would take one look
at me and that hardened heart of his would finally melt. I
was sure that this time he would tell me what I wanted to
hear—that I was his "pride and joy" and his "sweet pea." I
was sure that this time he would run to greet me, sweep me
up in his arms and squeeze me so tight that I just might have
popped if he hadn't stopped.*

That was the way things unfolded—in my imagination, back then, when I was a five year old child. But sadly, it was only make-believe. As much as I wanted it to happen, as much as I prayed that it would happen, it didn't happen that way. Not with my Father, Martin McBride. When that self-important college professor pulled up in the driveway in his new sports car, I knew right away from the look on his face that he was in his own little world again—preoccupied with work and worry and whatever else middle-aged men think about. And so, when he walked through the door and I ran to greet him, he looked straight through me as if I were not even in the room. He didn't give me the time of day. Father passed me by and headed straight for his office without so much as speaking a word.

As the memory of that day came into my consciousness, waves of strong emotion washed over me like billows in the turbulent sea. I felt it from the top of my head to the tip of my toes—heartbreaking rejection and an agonizing sense that I was not and never would be worthy of love.

Another memory came into my awareness. Like on a movie screen before me, I saw all of the scenes from Mark's sermons roll by one by one. Hellfire and damnation. Wailing and gnashing of teeth. Rolling waves of molten lava. Demons spewing fire from their nostrils like angry medieval dragons. Even though it had happened so long ago, I was there. In the moment. In the trauma. In the fear. Terrified that God was my worst enemy. My accuser.

And as I got in touch with those feelings in all of their intensity, I began to weep uncontrollably. I was just a young seeker, an impressionable little girl whose relationship with God was clouded by the man who introduced me to an angry God. There they were, surfacing, those terrible archetypes of the mean deity. And so, at twenty-something years old, the child in me was grieving—grieving profuse, hot, wet tears for all of the years of my life that were lost while I was wandering in a spiritual wilderness—so lost and alone. I cried for what seemed like hours until I was completely spent, drained—exhausted.

But in the midst of that grief, something miraculous happened. As in a vision, in my mind's eye, I saw a figure appear in the distance. Coming ever closer, a man was standing at the top of a hill. Hazy and unrecognizable at first, he was enveloped in light. Drawn by his presence, I saw myself run to meet him.

Then, face to face, I saw Him. His eyes were glowing with love as bright as a flame of fire. There was a magnetic presence all about Him. I knew in a moment who He was....

It was Jesus.

Suddenly, the air surrounding us was thick and smelled fragrant like incense. As Jesus stood before me, I saw now for the first time His beauty, His compassion and His mercy. His face was radiant, shining with the love of God as He spoke these words…

I have loved you with an everlasting love, Maggie;
with lovingkindness I have drawn you.

There He was—Jesus, tender, yet strong and mighty. Majestic, and yet humble. My eyes were fixed on Him, enraptured by His presence. There was no flaw in Him. He was more beautiful than anything that my mind had ever, or would ever imagine. He was breathtaking as fiery love continued to burn in His eyes.

I am Jesus. Your Savior, your Redeemer, your Beloved.

In that holy moment, after hearing His voice, I heard the sound of a heavenly choir. The music filled me with such longing as the words penetrated by heart…

Come, ye sinners, poor and needy,
Weak and wounded, sick and sore;

Jesus ready stands to save you,
Full of pity, love and power.
I will arise and go to Jesus,
He will embrace me in His arms;
In the arms of my dear Savior,
O there are ten thousand charms.

As I began to weep, I could feel my heart of stone softening because of His amazing love. The Lord was saving me, healing me, drawing me to Himself. Drawing me with His lovingkindness. Drawing me with His compassion. Christ the Savior had transcended time, and was embracing my brokenness and touching the pain of my childhood with His tender mercies and healing love. Even though I was sitting on my sofa, even though I was present to the earthly dimension, I could feel His heavenly presence all around me. I could hear the gentle voice of Jesus say...

Ask me for what you will, Maggie, ask and you will receive.

My heart leapt within me at the sound of His voice. In an instant, my any lingering unbelief was transformed into faith. From the depths of my spirit I cried out: "Heal me. Bring me out of my loneliness. Touch my heart, Jesus. Touch my heart."

The nearness of Him becoming more and more captivating, I could actually feel Him laying His hands upon this heart of mine that had been broken over and over by my own sins and the sins of others—this heart that had been captive to loneliness and isolation all of my life. This heart that had been hiding from love.

And when He did, when He touched my heart, it felt like a bolt of lightning ran through me. My soul felt electric—like a mighty rushing stream coursing through my veins while I basked in His healing presence.

I heal the brokenhearted,
and bind up their wounds.

Still in a vision, the best part was yet to be. Jesus, abounding with love and kindness looked deeply into my eyes, took my hand in his and laid it upon *His* chest. And when He did, I could not only feel, but also hear the song of His heart...resounding in Him, resounding in me. The longing that He had for a close relationship with me—the heavenly choir was singing once more...

> *Come, ye thirsty, come, and welcome,*
> *God's free bounty glorify;*
> *True belief and true repentance,*
> *Every grace that brings you nigh.*
> *I will arise and go to Jesus,*
> *He will embrace me in His arms;*
> *In the arms of my dear Savior,*
> *O there are ten thousand charms.*

And so, there in that moment, in that very room, Jesus *had* embraced me in His arms. I sensed for the first time I was free indeed. Free from bitterness. Free from shame. Free from loneliness. Most of all, free from the fear of God that had held me captive all of my life.

His perfect love had truly cast out my fear.

I knew in my heart that from that day forward, I could reach out to God with the trusting heart of a child and He would embrace me in return. God had lavished His love on me that day and I would never be the same again. Nothing would be able to separate me from His love. Not death or angels or demons, or things that might trouble me in the present, or things that have wounded me in the past. Nothing in all creation would ever be able to separate me from the love of God in Christ Jesus.

No more feeling like a rejected little girl inside. No more fatherlessness. I belonged to Him.

With my eyes still closed, and for the first time, I saw Jesus as He really is—a kind Shepherd who tenderly cares for His sheep—the Son of God who came to fulfill His mission.

Hear the words of the Lord:

> *The Spirit of the Lord is on me, because he has anointed me*
> *to preach good news to the poor. He has sent me to heal the*
> *brokenhearted, to proclaim release to the captives, recovering*
> *of sight to the blind, to deliver those who are crushed...*

Indeed, God had begun the process of healing His brokenhearted daughter. As comforted as His presence made me feel, I didn't want that moment to end. But realizing that I couldn't remain in His glory forever, Jesus kissed me on my forehead and then turned to walk back up the hill. And as He departed, He left me with a promise:

> *Now I will lead you with chords of human kindness, with ties of love; I will lift the yoke from your neck and bend down to feed you. I will not carry out my fierce anger on you, nor devastate you, Maggie, for I am God and not man—I am the Holy one among you.*

And so, in that bleak December, on that unforgettable night, I received an early Christmas present—a vision of Christ and His unfailing love. The song that the carolers sang on the streets of Birmingham finally had meaning for me…

> *Joy to the world, the Lord is come*
> *Let earth receive her King*
> *Let every heart, prepare Him room*
> *And Heaven and nature sing!*
> *And Heaven and nature sing!*
> *And Heaven and nature sing!*

My heart, this stony heart, had finally prepared Him room and now I was feeling *joyful* for the first time in my life. The Lord had come to me and I received Him as Savior and King.

And so, with my burdens lifted and joy in my heart, I anticipated the old year coming to a close and the New Year dawning like a glorious, golden sunrise above the horizon. The mistakes and failures of my yesterdays would eventually be distant memories. The ache of fatherlessness was all gone. The pain had been soothed by the warmth of the everlasting arms of my Savior.

Faith was rising up in me. True faith. I could feel it. Sense it. Faith that anticipated the good to come. Faith that expected a future bright with promise.

> *For I, the Lord, know the plans that I have for you, plans for peace and not disaster, tragedy or adversity— I have plans to give you a future filled with fresh hope.*

And so, dear reader, after all this time, after all the years of seeing through a glass darkly, the eyes of my heart had *finally* been opened to the truth a church girl *can* talk about.

God is not mad at me after all.

Acknowledgments

Well, now that all y'all have read my book, I need to do what Mama Dot (my mother) taught me to do and "give credit where credit is due."

For starters, I'd like to give a big Southern "thank you very much" to Bill Alverson, proof reader extraordinaire. Mr. Alverson spent untold hours on this project, going over the manuscript with a fine-tooth comb trying to decipher the charming southernisms from just piss-poor English. I thank you from the bottom of my heart, Bill, and hope that it is everything that you had hoped it would be now that the project is over. You are patient and meticulous. For that, I am eternally grateful.

I'd also like to thank my ninety-year-old mother, Dorothy Nell and my daddy, James Maxwell, who has gone to be with Jesus. Without being raised by these folks from Guin, Alabama, I would not have had a quiver full of Southern sayings with which to bring to this work of fiction.

No acknowledgement would be complete without mentioning my loved ones and friends who make my life sweet. Thanks to my husband, John, and my daughter, Annie Nell, for their encouragement and willingness to roll with my obsessions, one of which is writing. I love you both. Secondly, thanks to my precious girlfriends whom I also love and cannot do without, not even for one day—DeAnn, Gayle and Karen. Y'all are precious!

It is my hope that the folks who read this novel will be entertained and healed through humor. After all, as Harry Ward Beecher said, "Mirth is God's best medicine."

From bittersweet, home Alabama,
Susan Sieweke
"Suzelle"

188

NOTES:

All sermons, hymns, quotes, songs and poetry used in this novel are in the public domain except for the copyrighted songs and poetry written by the author, Susan Sieweke: "Child Out in the Rain," "Healing Love," "The Prosperity Dance," "The Narcissistic Blues," "Who You Are," "The Coffee Shop," and "Song for the Prodigal: You Belong to Me."

All scripture references are taken from the King James Version of the Bible (also in the public domain) and upon occasion, reworded by the author to fit the story line.

The author has also taken creative liberties as to time, place, and other details when writing about Birmingham, Alabama, AZO pills and Ibuprofen.

Works in the public domain in order of appearance in the novel are:
"Just as I Am," Charlotte Elliott, 1835.
"Sinners in the Hands of an Angry God," Jonathan Edwards, 1741.
Much Ado About Nothing, William Shakespeare, 1599.
"Softly and Tenderly," Will L. Thompson, 1880.
"Joy to the World," Isaac Watts, 1719.
"Come Gracious Spirit, Heavenly Dove," Simon Browne 1720.
"Come Ye Sinners, Poor and Needy," Joseph Hart, 1759.

ABOUT THE AUTHOR

Susan Sieweke was raised by Mama Dot, who taught her to bake banana bread, shell butter beans and drink sweet tea with the best of Southern women. During the day, Susan works with the homeless as a Program Manager at the University of Alabama at Birmingham for the EARTH Day Treatment Program. At night, she studies law at Birmingham School of Law. Susan is also a musician and songwriter. She and her husband, John, live in Alabama with their four-legged critters. This is her first novel. To visit the authors website go to www.susansieweke.com.